AF783686

DISCOVERY OF DIVINITY WITHIN
From a Personal File

About the Author

With an out-of-the-ordinary insight in hand Sourin Banerji has made a wonderful foray into the innermost anatomy of his self to find the window on divinity within. It is his wont, too, only honed by his journalistic proficiency that has helped pave the way to realization.

His perceptions and experience coming into focus through autobiographical events aided by those of others around him all his life are variegated yet rich enough to make his insight all the more appealing.

His information management in two English newspapers of the ABP group, Kolkata, besides two other Bengali dailies, also publihed from the city, has earned him fame as an applied journalist.

Banerji was a visting faculty for over 20 years in journalism at Calcutta University from which he took his M.A. and LL.B. He also served the communication college of Bharatiya Vidya Bhavan as a coordinator. As a Thomsonian scholar he visited Britain.

Several of his professional works are textbooks in honours and post-graduate courses in journalism.

This profitable interaction in the outer world has much helped the author go in for an empirical communion with the inmost divinity. His personal file written in an overly intimate style with a philosophical bent greatly smoothes out the run-up to conceptual sublimation.

DISCOVERY OF DIVINITY WITHIN
From a Personal File

SOURIN BANERJI

CONCEPT PUBLISHING COMPANY, NEW DELHI - 110059

All rights reserved. No part of this work may be reproduced, stored in a retrieval system, or transmitted in any form or by any means, electronic, mechanical, photocopying, microfilming, recording or otherwise, without the prior written permission of the copyright owner and the publisher.

ISBN 81-7022-954-5

First Published 2002

© Author

Published and Printed by

Ashok Kumar Mittal
Concept Publishing Company
A/15-16, Commercial Block, Mohan Garden,
NEW DELHI -110059 (India)

Phones : 5351460, 5351794
Fax : 091-11-5357103
Email: publishing@conceptpub.com

My Pronams

Sri Ramakrishna

Srima Sarada

Swami Vivekananda

ALL power is within you;
you can do anything and everything.
(...power is there – potential or manifest it is there....)

You can do anything and everything
without even the guidance of anyone.
All power is there. Stand up
and express the divinity within you.

***

MAN is to become divine by realising the divine.

***

EACH soul is potentially divine.
The goal is to manifest this divinity within,
by controlling nature, external and internal.

– Swami Vivekananda

PROLOGUE

This is not just a life-story of mine, that of a diminutive individual who is much like a common run of men often obsessed with ordinary ambitions but seldom capable of towering other humans.

Neither is it a mere pleasure trip of mine into nonsense realms hemmed around by a closed-door circuit, me trying to hide desire and dirt under the carpet.

No such perverted intention do I have, and anyone can take an inquisitive look inside to see if I am doing it.

The search within will not reveal any blotch, even if imaginary; contrarily, the revelation will be something that puts me on an untrodden track of life, something with an extraordinary bent longing for the heavenly sunshine.

But it does not mean I am the image of a man infinitely blessed since muddy patches of clouds now and then darken the horizon and my rainbow vision.

At this old age of mine I do not like to play any hide-and-seek game with the searcher if there is one. It will be too childish to be a playmate with anybody. The access road to my room is wide open. All people can come inside to judge if I am talking all bosh.

My long life is full of queer feelings often richly honed by perceptions which have several times hoisted me to a height ironically taller than that of a dwarf but never making me a demonic nuisance.

Is it not the divine bliss? Humbly, it is. The growth whatever in my life is better than normal as is evident in human beings. It will not be one too many if I say I have often crossed the limits to go beyond man.

Most of our people are abject existentialists, their attachment to the family and society holding them back. They are blocked midway to their freedom with little hope for stepping out of the bondage.

Ground realities of their environs generally make them egocentric earthlings barring their entry into the blissful kingdom.

Ever on my toes, though, I do not claim I fully succeeded in overstepping all spoilsports in life, but howsoever my failings are, have only superficially blunted my divine spells.

Still the queer something in me has been highly stimulating, the criss-cross currents of my seemingly flashy wanderings undergoing more than skin-deep changes.

Flashy thoughts are related to earthy man and society while deep ones produce a spiritual bent in the thinking of man as an individual. And this individuality, when blessed by divine unfoldment, becomes spirituality.

Being is becoming which underlines the holy truth of character revolution, the kind of a socialised transformation that excites the manifestation of divinity within individuals.

Divinity is everywhere – in you, me, and all; yet our individual perceptions vary depending on manifold discoveries. Destinations remain distant for many of us, still searches are on.

My reflective searches have always been steadfast, for I have the feeling that character building, the key to man-making for attaining divine wisdom, is not done in a day. Realization is not easy-sailing.

The journey to divinity is oftentimes beset with vicissitudes, some unpredictable and some man-made, the barricades popping out here and there unwittingly, and the bang suddenly takes people offguard.

The routine life-style falls short of the required pep for character building, a normal feature with many people who go by the stream blindfoldedly, almost floating like water hyacinths hiding the divine water underneath; but mine is a different life put in a slot that waits to be dug up.

Even then my life is not an unmixed good. There are successes, there are failures. Predicaments are neither too few. Still all such situations together have done a lot good to me paving the run-up to a borderland where the earthly green mixes up with the heavenly blue.

To me it has been a bliss, born of a euphoric sojourn into divinity.

But not all has been good. Oppressive itches and possessive discomfitures have sometimes got the better of the good and thrown my sublime life into disarray. Still I have held the fort and braved the weather, feeling within me a kind of tectonical movements always propelling my physio-psycho progress.

Never would I claim I have been a perfect explorer and discoverer of divinity within, yet now and then I have had smart showers of the desired bliss.

My conscience is inviolable, its firm expression inspiring greatly the spirit of an inner-line gutsy transformation into understanding what the bliss is all about. All people may have this innate power of understanding, but they do not possess the right will to use it properly to be able to jump the pervasive egoism and know themselves.

Knowing the divinity in man is a trying job, but when it is done it reveals the universal truth of human equation in all its glory. Life is love that is divine, but can all the humans solve this enigmatic question?

Perhaps, a spiritual mindset stands behind the fleeting tryst with divinity. It is subjectivity, an individual notion that is too powerful to make the thrust into discovery. How many people do have the mundane motivation for godly perception? What then?

Religion being the manifestation of divinity in man I can humbly ask how many people are rightly directed towards the goal of life. Are we to blame it on lack of proper search within? Does it require a strong intellectual power to come near to the ethereal concept of divinity?

All men are equal in having divinity within but are unequal in attaining it. It all depends on the capability of individuals. And therein lies the difference, for which individual attainments are different.

The realization is mind-friendly, but where is the mind in the human anatomy and can it be located as other organs are?

But mind exists, not in the body but in the idea, the idea of commingling of three sense organs – brain, heart and stomach.

Do all these get us the soul, the immortal *atman* found in every existence making all beings equal?

This Vedantic derivative speaks of the basic unity of man, but the fact of life is the equality levels are different having been determined by individual capabilities. Yet the soul is the meeting point.

Man can start off from this point to get at the divine elevation which alone can help in man-making.

Not with pride, but with humility, I may say I have tried to be an exception all my life to get the result of my ardent research. The sayings and writings of world-seers I have read with a scanning eye; and I have duly noted the relative attainments of individual persons; and for this I can profess I can measure with my proficiency the extent of universal oneness.

Divinity is one, realizations manifold. So I am not sore with the idea that my realizations will not be similar to those of others. And so also will the levels of attainments be variable.

Still my own perceptions and realizations are worlds away from illusions, because my zeal for the blissful unfoldment has been real, unalloyed by fake showmanship.

The bliss, when any, may not be lasting; the flicker of divinity within may have looked like a wavering light in the darkness around; yet never have I been in a hurry to board the bus to blessings. In good spirits I have moved along the rough road and whenever blessings came, I just humbly welcomed them. Then it has been a wonder.

The years of my life are not too often green, yet the silver linings in the surrounding light and shade have shown me the ways towards the abiding love for man although its day-to-day manifestations have been dissimilar, sometimes disappointing. But I have not given in.

Odds have been against me in my formative days; the forward days have been hazy full of kinks and knots often jolting me to the knees; and the latter course of my life is long-winded, hazards alternating with hopes, despairs with joy. Ups and downs seem to go along with blisses and banes.

But I have never been bothered about doom, since my desire for divine homework has been too intensively honest.

Some occasional silly follies and foibles of mine have thrown me into utter debris, but astoundingly the same keen desire has come up to salvage me from the doom. Facing the music and paying through the nose are routine challenges. I have met them squarely, seldom budging from the path charted for me by my destiny.

It has been discipline that stands me in my stride and this noble quality I have learnt in my early academic times, for which my life-songs are never a chorus in the wilderness.

Man changes environment, so does environment to man—forever a two-way traffic on which I am never a loner, and like-minded there are several of the humans. But, unfortunately, many are weaklings, if servile.

Modestly, I am not of this type with the little intention of surrendering to the evil. Instead, the changing environs have only steeled my mind to sing aloud 'I shall overcome'.

With fortitude I have got over the waves, though sometimes I have been adrift in the ocean of dismay. Never done in I am. I see the hand of divine berth ashore.

The micro-macro analysis of my life helps me to know what I am. Several personal anecdotes and episodes commingle with my impersonal thoughts all generously contributing towards the revolution of my character, not much pronounced yet not too negligible. Explorative diggings into within have reacted splendidly steam-hammering my rocky transition from child-to-old days.

My village where I was born is not the same old face. Today it is urban-oriented. Neither is the city where I have grown up the same old. It is now a sprawling megacity.

Everywhere amateurishness is gone. Hi-tech cyber professionalism catches on. Citizens, rural or urban, are more candid than before.

The rapids of change are more visibly notable in the city than in the village pushing newer values to the driver's seat. Egos crane their necks high – on ethos. The road to divinity is thus bumpy.

Admittedly, the book on divine pursuits has some autobiographical embellishments prompted by innermost urges for lofty thinking, but my fear is this bold outspokenness may give rise to certain inordinate misconceptions blurring the line of fulfillment.

What else can I do? All study materials have been selectively picked up from my personal file for corroboration of my sincere intentions.

Not a heliography this volume either, which signals only the bright side of a character. The narratives here related to my life are purposefully tuned to expressing both the divinity and adversity.

This 'bio-diversity' volume has given same weights to sordid aberrations, sorrowful abrasions, humble feats, and glorified achievements, all neatly woven into a readout. Whatever the derivatives and imperatives, are only modest inputs used to clear the decks for divine digging. I have tried to make a balanced appraisal of my positive and negative sides.

Segmented though, my entire life underlines an orderly development from dawn to evening.

The pursuits branch off into learning and teaching, romantic aura and political activism, and social work, professional writings and extensive travelling. And now the retired life is both sweet and sour.

Above all, the motivations behind all my endeavours have been blessed with a democratic fervour, bereft of rabid dogmatism. It is possibly the divinity within me that has perforce directed me in growing as a social revolutionary and in honing my journalistic perfection.

But I have never been tension-free, and till the evening time of my life Dame Luck is not smiling. Can divine sedatives give me the blissful sunshine?

What I have learnt is the mindset has to be so tuned as to track divinity everywhere in this planet earth. The earth is the only place where the heaven and the hell co-exist making the feeling of one with oneness a divine truth.

CONTENTS

My Thanks

Mr. G.K. Dutt

Dr. L.N. Banèrjee

Mr. N.N. Mukherjee

Prof. S.L. Mukherjee

Mr. A.B. Patra

Mrs. Indira Banerjee

Mr. Kishore Banerjee

Mr. Saumya Bandyopadhyay

Mr. Arya Bandyopadhyay

Mr. A.K. Mittal

Mr. Ashim Das

1

FORMATIVE DAYS

In the formative days of my life, more often than not, was I in deep waters adrift like a straw on the waves lashed by the wind, seldom knowing whither was I moving. And it was all surprise whenever the wavy crescendo threw me out into the sandy shore.

There I could take heart of grace, the divine grace, wasn't it?

My love's labour was it, at times lost, though. Yet I must confess I did get the blessings now and again. Or were they not the occasional manifestations of divinity within?

My inmost feelings have frequently been mixed with the heaven-hell earthliness,the undulating terrain being the upshot of seemingly hegemonistic socialised milieu. My successes and failures are but natural.

Foolhardy snobbery was not my forte. Never has it been so. The curtain of obscurantist nonchalance has not been my hiding place. A selfless truth-seeker, I have made constant efforts not to indulge in excercises in orthodox fantasy or in modern high-flown idiosyncracy.

All kinds of ballooning manoeuvres have been ineffective, and I stand rock-ribbed, never on quick-sand.

My life seems forever trouble-torn; seldom is it easy-going. And I have not taken the leap into the unknown, though the known surroundings – the hills, the plains, the skies and the seas – have stood before me as blockades. Still I cannot remain satisfied with the traditional fatalism. Earnestly have I tried to get at 'I am, I am,' which is less than an apology of the soul-stirring omni-I-am'.

Isn't it ignorance? It is, a kind of it. But ignorance was bliss when I was born. The village environ then did not permit a baby-in-arms to learn more than the cradle-life, swinging to and fro in blessed ecstasy.

A cow-shed in our village home was my birthplace. Strangely today, but not at that time when nursing homes did not mushroom in numbers. A cow-shed used to be considered then as the most disinfected labour room.

Charghat is the name of the village, situated in Basirhat subdivision now of north 24-Parganas district, then forty miles north-east of Kolkata, negotiable by boat or cart from the railway station Maslandpur or Gobardanga on the Bongaon line of EBR, now ER.

Living though miles away from the city we were not literally village folks; rather, we did not have the kind of rustic outlook that was common at that time. All were by and large educated and had the mind to move to the city for work and settlement. But few could think of deserting the sylvan root. My father Nagendranath Banerji and uncle Sailendranath stayed in the city and became virtually week-enders and at the wee hours of our life we would look forward to their blessed home-coming.

Two years after my birth I got another brother Satindranath and again after two years' interval yet another brother Sukumar was born. A good family it was, with divine smiles showering on us. But then all of a sudden misfortune overtook us. What went wrong I did not know; I was too young to decipher the divine code; but I got it by heart that divinity had eluded us.

My mother Sukumari died when I was four and a half years old and the youngest one was only six months old. Mother died of malignant malaria in just a day before any medical help could reach her. Only one MBBS doctor was there at that time, away at Gobardanga, and as he came he found a pretty youthful lady lying dead, pale and white.

God was so unkind! But we the brothers did not know what had befallen us. We looked at her from a distant and then slipped away into hiding, with tears rolling down our soft cheeks. Sukumar slept.

Father was away in the city; after getting the death news he hurried home. He looked glum, but took courage for making arrangements for cremation.

Crawling out of the hiding I stood behind our neighbours to peep at my mother lying motionless draped in a red-bordered *sari* on the open verandah, her eyes closed and hands stretched. It was death divine! I was sad she did not give me that last hug. I felt my younger brother had come. And then we ran away when it was time to lift the body of my mother on an improvised bier.

Who did the last rites by the river Yamuna that flows by our village, I do not remember, even today. I have not dared to ask anyone. Probably, the divine grace had saved us from dousing our burning eyes.

The mourning over, the *sradh* ceremony was performed. Our heads were shaved clean, but did we do the ritual?

Sheer neglect took the life of our youngest brother. Was his life too short to be divine? Only after six months he left us for good. We were awe-struck but did not cry.

Under fatherly care we the two young children grew up. Widowers were wont to re-marry, but my father did not do that and bring us a new mother. Blissfully, we were spared the step-motherly neglect.

At the village *pathsala* we began our study. There were mud walls and a thatched roof above that adorned the old-styled school. We used to sit within cubicles, the refrain of our mumbles creating an uproar. The grey-haired lanky *panditmashai* would hold a bamboo stick and beat when we failed to answer him. At times we were made to kneel down with our heads low and holding two bricks in two hands. Out of fear we learnt our lessons and the discipline associated with it. Our upbrining now appears foolproof.

Both the brothers joined a city school in Kolkata as we grew up. Cousin sister Santilata Mukherjee was with us all the early years and her motherly care got us through.

My father and uncle were then residing in rented houses. Sudhindranath and Sukhendranath were two sons of my uncle and they were studying in the same school with us. My father was a teacher in mathematics endowed with an extraordinary flair in the subject while my uncle was an office-hand.

Altogether we were four brothers, and no sister. Under the same roof we grew up playing, studying and quarrelling, yet bound by one divine love.

During school vacations we would go to the village home but our other two brothers did not accompany us usually. Why was it so? The reason was unknown. So missing was the divine grace.

Our village house that would remain locked for months on end was a pucca building. Recently it has been renovated. But in those days, when we entered the premises, we had to duster and wash it clean to make it habitable. Sometimes we could not get a cook when we had to arrange for our meals in neighbouring houses. That way we covered almost all the households.

Some landed property we had. My father expanded the horizon at the instance of my grandma. Everything went well until the government acquisition. Father died in 1961, almost a broke. The compensation money came to our pocket after decades.

Age-old relations in the village changed with the handing of lands to ryots. But none could be singled out for effecting the change. It came over collectively, through the panchayati raj and its concomitant reforms. There occurred a generation gap.

We were in rainy days, battered by storms, throwing us in disarray, after the death of my father. But the silver lining was that my brother had by then become a doctor, earning our livelihood. I was not earning at first, but later conscience pricked me and I decided to jump into the bandwagon of money-spinners though very marginally.

Our villagefolks were by and large poor, and this gave me some consolation. No matter if we did not have two meals a day. What mattered much was we had to keep the family together.

I was feeling ill at ease at home, but my pre-occupations with things other than family feeding were itching me all the time. Yet I was tied hand and foot. Where would I get the escape route from poverty and misery? Would not Dame Luck favour me?

To my wonder I found some families were doing well as the social-economic fabric changed with the times.

And there was a change in the traditional feudalistic system of things, the trend being towards a democratic orientation. The increased human interaction resulted from educational advancement. Still, I did find, the non-egoistic homogeneity remained a far cry. What a little good that had come was the minimal bond of togetherness.

Behind this bond was the hand of a few devoted young men of the village all bubbling with the urge for doing good to society, and I, being too obsessed with our financial insufficiency in meeting both ends meet, readily decided to join the welfare work.

Charghat Milan Mandir was the name of the small club which spared no pains to develop the village by organising a school, a library, a co-operative, a health centre and a metalled road to Maslandpur railway station. Besides, sporting and recreational activities were organised. Football competitions got off to a flying start; theatres and *jatras* had enormous soothing effects on the monotony of life. The library Jogesh Pathagar was named after the actor-playwright Jogesh Chandra Chowdhury who belonged to the village. Also was remodelled the decades-old community temple where the Durga Puja used to be pompously performed. Nearby, in a village called Dargah, the Thakurbar Dargah was also rebuilt and refined.

Behind most of these achievements were the untiring and inspiring efforts by the political father figure of the village, Prafullanath Banerjee. My salute, my bow!

The marketplace was no more than a village *haat,* but nowadays it is the hub of centralised activity, people from far and near coming, jostling and roaring for making bargains. The Yamuna river flows by till today, but it has lost its idyllic charm of the olden days all because of silting and mud. The river, by the way, originates, from Tribeni in the Hooghly and flows into the Ichhamati.

In days of yore our regular pastime was to bathe in the placid river waters for hours, swimming avoiding the nets of fishermen, under the green shadows of branching mango trees and drooping and waving bamboos. Often did we dive deep into the river to touch the bed and swim like fish over it sometimes scratching our noses. A laughable fun it was. And a cooling bliss.

Neighbouring fishermen did not mind our taking their boats out for rowing far into the bend where the river was about to throw herself into the big arms of the Ichhamati. Sometimes we would sit on the banks for angling. All this was sheer happiness and divine.

Most of us were teenagers, all prankish youngsters playing at noon, slipping into gardens in the afternoon, and at sundown we just bagged some fruits or flowers to celebrate our home-coming. Even *nastachandra*, though often rewarded with beatings, was a divine cheer.

All these pranks gave me enough of diversions, and I enjoyed forgetting the family hunger. But as I grew up, and similarly others too, I found these had some sobering effect on the mind. The bygone times would not return, but it is a great pleasure in going down memory lane, however sweet or sour.

2

ROMANTIC AURA

The noontime of my life was yet to come, yet I was feeling some changes were going on within me. Was I growing old? Was I losing the life-verve? Out of fear I took the plunge into the core of my anatomy, and to my surprise I discovered the same divinity a little more vibrant than before in the same niche of ethereal life.

And that is the divine blessing I have not lost. Because it is the delight that helps to create a romantic aura around me.

Today, at this ripe age I look at the young boys and girls with awe, and in wonder. Are they less romantic? Is it premature adulthood?

But my budding life, though not easy-sailing, was dreamy. What the dreams were I do not recollect; nor can I at this forgetful age. But, certainly, I did not live with an eclipsed sun, neither with the fullmoon. The sun, even if eclipsed, would burn me to death; and I had no intention of getting bewilderingly moonstruck.

My jump, however, to the youthful age was bumpy, yet not unromantic. And my romantic rendezvous began with a love affair. Strangely, I forgot the cash nexus in my family.

During one *puja* vacation I went to my village where I met Usha, then a playful damsel, beaming with smile all the while of the day.

This chance meeting sparked romanticism in me, and I was sure such an affair did get divine bliss or else I would not have held on to her till date. In real life it matured into lasting companionship. And everything else in my village appeared to me all lovingly mine.

The romanticism also produced in me a kind of impulse to do social good. Our rural life was steeped in darkness despite some stray enlightening works done by our seniors. My romantic zeal helped me to cut a dash in development work.

Never was I tradition-bound. Somehow I began venting progressive feelings, the romantic in me only whetting my motivation. Political baptism though I had a little already, I stayed away with care from political activism. Social good became my target and with an unfailing vehemence I went my way.

Activities mainly centred round sports, music, theatre, and worship. Not a backbencher, nor in the front rank, mine was a mediocre versatility, and merrily did I participate in football, cricket, badminton, basketball and volleyball, besides swimming. Even I played tennis ball on village paths and city streets. But football, by divine grace, was in my blood.

In performing arts I made a mark, be that in stage theatre and singing. My acting drew applause, whether in Rabindranath's *Bisarjan* or in Tarasankar's *Kalindi.*

We did not have any permanent stage in our village; the set was improvised every time we performed. 'Dada' Anil Banerjee gave us the impetus, but he was an angry man often leaving us in the lurch yet coming back soon glum-faced.

Jogesh Chowdhury's *Sita* we staged but our performances did not match the pride of the playwright.

The sun-up or the sun-down I would sing full-throated and my village friends were all keen listeners. I was crazy about Pankaj Mullick's *Rabindra Sangeet,* but the modern songs by Kazi Najrul, Jaganmay Mitra, Dhananjay Bhattacharya and Hemanta Mukhopadhyay were my favourites.

The Durga Puja became the principal worship. It was a community *puja* in which all villagers took part. Drum-beating mixed with conchshell-blowing turned all *puja* evenings into blissful moments, and the mother goddess would look at us from divine heights.

And through the holy haze created by the burning of incense sticks the faces of divine idols looked bright and living.

Yet my romantic eyes were earthy, though very sublime. I had been looking as well for moving eyes of my sweetheart, from a distance, standing well behind the thronging crowd still with folded hands.

My romantic mind would soon take the flight of ecstatic fancy into the crescent moon shining above trees and clouds. I lost the track of the pretty face among the 'gals and pals' all engrossed in meditative moods.

Why was I so fickle and restive when *artis* were pompously performed? Perhaps, divinity escaped for a breather outside.

The sun-up *pushpanjali* and the sun-down *arti* were the two main draws during the *puja*. And, especially, the *arti* performed by uncle Santosh Kumar Chatterjee was a real treat for the eye and mind, while the *pushpanjali mantras* chanted by cousin *dada* Satyendranath used to reverberate through the *mandap* sending out the refrain into surrounding houses and woods.

All the villages and its folk stood divine!

In religion, there was no animosity, there was only amity, the *sine qua non* of our countryside life. Neither was there war of words among the *gurus* and *maulavis*. Making political mileage from communal ill feelings was virtually a taboo. We all lived together.

Thakurbar Dargah, a little distance away from the *puja mandap*, still represents the eternal unity of man. The *dargah* is the *samadhi* of a saintly Brahmin Thakurbar Bandyopadhyay, who lived during the reign of Hari Saha, a sunri by caste, a small bhuinya independent of mighty Pratapaditya. Hari, as the legend has it, fought his last ditch battle against Man Singh, the famous commander of Emperor Akbar.

The saint was brought up by a kind Muslim family of the village Dargah. Thakurbar preached God is one and used to wear *dhoti* like a *lungi*, unlike a Brahmin, and this practice created a confusion which resulted in his upbringing the Muslim way. Not only that, his death too raised a flutter among the Hindus and Muslims in villages around. The Hindus demanded that he be cremated while the Muslims wanted to bury him. The air was heavy.

But soon a rapprochement was reached between the contenders. His body was buried in a tomb with the sacred thread girdling it. This arrangement holds good today. And the Hindus offer *pujas* while the Muslims perform them.

Divinity, in the form of wisdom, prevails. The place is a pilgrim centre. All good or bad things happening in villages are made known to 'the tomb with the thread', indeed, for blessings.

Worship is divine, devotion is universal.

Like all other newly-wed couples, Usha and myself both visited the *dargah* for blessings after our wedding. Even, afterwards, we did the *manat* as our daughter-in-law was taken seriously ill. So do all others, whether ill or in fine shape.

It is secularism at its peak. And it is my firm belief, if not of all, this divine grace will be ever lasting and all pettyfogging, religious or political, will not succeed in demolishing the solid foundation of unity. *Dargah* may be a small place, but it epitomises the great life divine.

Am I echoing what Swami Vivekananda and Sri Aurobindo have said in their holy preachings?

Is it not one God, one man, one love?

Sai Baba of Shirdi has also talked about divine equation. Divinity is everywhere – within and without, and the bliss is in abundance waiting for the humans to pick up.

My romantic urge has often goaded me to delve deep into my anatomy or roam about in the open green-and-blue scenario, in search of the blessed root.

Early in the morning I would get up form my bed and slip out of doors to see the sun-bath of wavy paddy fields or riverside *ghats*. Mornings were cool with soft breeze, the chirping birds coming out of their nests behind the foliage of trees and flying into the red horizon aglow with the rising ball.

My heart sang out, my mouth spell-bound.

I loved my country.

Was this patriotism? What is it all about now? At this old age I desire history repeats itself, but to my dismay I find there is little patriotism today, a kind of divine love that stems from within.

Will it be foolish to recapitulate what Swami Ranganathananda, now the president of the Ramakrishna Mission and Math, Belur, in Howrah, said bluntly during the celebration of one hundred years of the Chicage Parliament of Religions, held at the Indoor Stadium of Eden Gardens, by the sacred Ganga of Kolkata? The Swami said free India had sent patriotism out into exile. It was a thunderous uttering, like, though in a different vein, that of Swami Vivekananda, who had endeared the 'sisters and brothers' of America in his very first address to the world congregation.

Yet my own divine perception today tells of the brightest thought – Paradise is not lost!

3

ANOTHER WORLD

Father brought me to Kolkata to get me admitted into a high-rise city school, but I was not even a teenager then and my nostalgia for the *pathsala* days remained so strong that it took months to develop the sense of belonging to a new academic atmosphere. It was a long jump for me, still a child with a rustic mind.

But the romanticism ingrained in me from my morning years got me through the maze of life, the stick-carrot upbringing under the eyes of hard-nut *panditmashai* helping me to fit in with the changing world.

The discipline I had learnt was of help, yet romantic bent I did not lose. However, I cannot say now it was a bliss.

Years rolled by, and, eventually, I stood first as a school-leaver way back in 1941. A divine bliss it was. Certainly. So I decided to offer my humble prayers to Adya Ma, the Goddess Kali. I went to the place of pilgrimage at Adayapith, Ariadaha, near Dakshineswar, on the eastern bank of the river Hooghly (generally called Ganga). My cousin sister Kirandi accompanied me to the temple on an afternoon in mid-summer. I was sitting alone on the open verandah, just facing the deity, while 'didi' was away meeting sanyasins in the temple office. A short distance away, a young boy was singing some devotional Ramprasad song full-throated and melodiously. Musical refrain filled the air. I was in meditation, deep in sublime thoughts, occasionally opening my eyes to have an intent look at the dark yet bright face of Mother. Out of nowhere did appear a brahmachari dressed all white who stood before me asking me to concentrate on the third eye of the Goddess. I marked the third eye was made of gold. I looked back at the brahmachari, who then said all smiles, "If you can do it well, you'll find soon the room of the deity is in flames." He left me. And I then tried out what he had desired. In moments I had a trance, and the wonderful experience. My 'didi' came. I looked for the brahmachari. But nowhere could I locate him. Wasn't it again a bliss, shortlived though?

But I did not get blessings of my maths-prodigy father as I fared badly in the subject. I opted for arts, with a liking for civics. Then in the graduation course I had the honours in economics in which I got my master's degree with distinction.

Whatever literary flair did I have, was born of my latent romanticism, but the imaginative power of mine found outlets in writing on topics more akin to economics and politics. In 1948 I did M.A. and later in 1951 the LLB.

Prof. Benoy Sarkar, a giant teacher at that time, had wanted me to take up sociology as a special subject, but I did not heed him; instead I went in for banking and currency and I was a total flop. No blessings of God, ah!

My father had desired I would be a lawyer. For a year I was articled to a senior at the Calcutta High Court bar. But that, too, ended up in a fiasco. Under pressures from my family – I was married then – I had to leave law and join journalism as my profession. Not a divine grace!

By then I was in deep waters of politics although I did not join any political bandwagon. I stayed on with social work. Politics came as an aside in my run-up to higher education. Even so it was not a babu-type armchair fancy-fair; at the most it was student politics.

The 'Do or Die' slogan of the 1942 August Revolution was the first bite I took in politics, but it was only superficial even though I got a good beating by the British police at Wellington Square (now Subodh Mullick Square). I suffered a nagging pain in my back.

Stormy times marked my college years after my 1942 baptism, but never did I get fully involved in political activism. Still I developed some progressive thoughts prompted by my classmate, a veteran trade unionist, Kamalapati Roy, now dead. Cousin brother Basantalal Chatterjee, a terrorist then, a communist later, tried to be a pathfinder for me. But I did not relent. I did not allow my respect for Gandhiji, the mass- motivator, to get jolted; nor did I fail to hold Subhas Chandra Bose, not the Netaji by then, high in my esteem.

Some other progressives like former Calcutta University Vice-Chancellor Santosh Bhattacharya, Prof. Gautam Chattopadhyay and MP Mrs. Gita Mukherjee were all known fellow-travellers.

My rustic mind did not leave me even when I was a city-grown man. As a student of politics and economics I used to go out of the urban periphery to get familiar with peasants, and once I took part in their Tebhaga movement, far down in Basirhat subdivision, and got arrested along with five other students, one of them a girl. Captured we came to the Sandeshkhali thana for being taken to Basirhat court handcuffed.

Our shackles were removed to have dinner with the policeman on guard. We cut jokes; we discussed trifles. The dinner over, we all went in order to a nearby pond for wash. It was dark. Torches were lit. Suddenly the girl friend slipped and got stuck up in the mud. While pulling herself out one of her chappals went deep into the mire. She shouted out and tried to salvage it by stooping low but failed.

Surprisingly, then, one policeman put off his shoes and went knee-deep into water. The search was on and the chappal appeared soaked, the water dripping.

To my wonder it all happened in a moment. Was I wrong if I thought it was a manifestation of the divinity even within a captor? Hurriedly, I made a research work in my mind to get at the truth – that all men are equal, the captor and the captive, and that love is all gold that ever glitters.

We were huddled into a boat for our night journey to Hasnabad, a riverside town near Basirhat. Soon one or two of my friends started snoring. They were so tired. But I remained awake and until I slept I looked out of the small window of the boat, away into the star-studded sky. Was it bliss from the heaven that I wanted?

The boat was moving upstream with the tidal flow tossing it over the swift current of waters. The police were on the vigil. A boatman started singing, but not a *bhatiyali* it was. Still its refrain was sweet, numbing me to sleep in blissful peace.

Herded on the station platform and tied by ropes hand and waist, we got into a train. People around looked at us awe-stuck. In shackles though, my mind yelled romanticism as I sang out a patriotic song *sarthaka janama aamaar janmechhi ei deshe* (Blessed is my birth, I am born in this country) and soon it became a chorus.

Into the court lock-up we entered and waited there for our turn in appearing before the magistrate. We were granted the conditional bail – that we would not go to the Sandeshkhali area.

Not thus blessed by the divine hand we came out of the court and at once faced thousands of students who fired questions as to why we had accepted the conditional bail. Their strong disapproval of our virtual surrender stunned us dumb. They said about their plans for a bigger agitation for our release but that could not materialise for our docile attitude. We had no answer. Was it not a political blunder? But then we did not do politics with the misfortune of our *barga* farmers. Ours was a fraternal study tour. Yet my obsession hung around. And no blessing.

Sitting under an old banyan tree we were sipping tea when some sleuths surrounded us asking about our movements. We kept mum. They gave up.

The morning after, we left Basirhat. Silently, and to different destinations. I went to a friend's house at Kholapota, only a few miles away.

Early next day I boarded a bus to Maslandpur via Baduria, and from the station I walked up to my village Charghat to see my father.

As I came near our house I found my father was standing at the doorstep. It was awful. How did he come to know that I was coming? Probably, someone of my village had spotted me at the station and cycled home to inform my father earlier.

My father was in tears as he put his hand of bliss on my head and I bowed down to touch his divine feet.

Softly did he scold me, 'Why are you neglecting your study? Remember you are a good student and I expect good results from you.' I smiled. He said nothing more. We moved in.

Great Famine of Bengal, the war-day bane, had left a sorry stamp on my village and around; the starved people still stalking the land in utter convulsion. Friend Arun Banerjee, who later became a doctor and my relation, and I had then organised relief measures extensively with the help of the Hindu Mahasabha and People's

Relief Committee. After having tea with my father I just went out to see how the famished brethren were doing. They recognised me and expressed their anguish. I felt sorry for them; I could not end their sufferings. It was a blotch. Within me I did not find the divine sublimation.

Some club members, at an evening gathering, insisted on my shunning politics, but I categorically told them I did not do politics though sometimes my social commitments led me to the political whirlpool. Never did I part ways with my club, until my old age.

Milani was the mouthpiece of our club. I was its editor and Arun a columnist. Only a few issues saw the light and people in general liked them. But its life was short. I made an enquiry within. No bliss!

Even though I held some progressive ideas, I could not dwarf my romantic height. When I was home, I would move out and mix with people exchanging my ideas with them. Golam Ambia was a young friend of mine residing in an outlying village; he was the first man to appreciate my feelings and leanings. Later, he became a political activist while I remained aloof. Some of my brethren dubbed me a communist, but I told them I did not believe in any kind of dogmatic philosophy. Nor any science. I was averse to indoctrination.

My exams were near. My father wanted me to take a holiday from my extracurricular work. I did not disobey him and concentrated on academic exercises.

The only thing I had done in the meantime was I took part in the Azad Hind Fauz movement that swept the country from the Red Fort in Delhi to far-flung areas beyond the seas and hills. We missed the Netaji in person but his speeches, besides the INA hearings, were resounding in thunder. We missed him, no doubt; but his outstretched hand calling all of the Indians to march on Delhi could not be ignored. 'Delhi Chalo' and 'Jai Hind' were two blissful calls.

My search within revealed the Netaji had his ideological thrust from Swami Vivekananda's thoughts, but the disciple went in for political revolution while the *guru* kept away. Earlier, Chittaranjan Das had the inspiration from the Swami.

But interpretations were different, so the paths they followed differed. Bigotry never can have the divins pep.

4

TURNING POINT

The progressive tilt in my political model did never dampen my democratic and patriotic fervour. But I could not compromise with dogmatism. Whenever I came under attack from the hardliners of any brand, I fought them out. Being an Indian denizen how could I tolerate ideas imported either from the Soviet Union or from China? My thoughts on well-being did not thrive on borrowed ideas, a policy-frame that was different from the one of hardliners.

If nation-building depends on the prevailing objective conditions of a country, how can I support the determining factor that is suitable in other countries? I cannot be dissociated from home-ground conditions.

Freedom has come; will it make us up for the grabs whatever the consequences? The spoils left for us by the ruling nation cannot make us ignore the great potentials of our own soil. And what is to be done, then?

Our greed has brought us too many cooks who are spoiling the broth. No, this was not the idea when we cut across the barrier of dependence.

Sincerely did I hold on to the philosophy of socialism which had dawned on us way back in the Vedantic times and this philosophy had never been soiled by bloodbath. It was divine love. Obviously, I was influenced by this theory. Since, I was very much opposed to bloody revolution for creating a new social order. Swami Vivekananda's teaching was behind my thinking this way.

But confusion prevailed on me when I heard the Swami speak on religious explosion for the birth of socialism. How can this religious explosion bring about a lasting change is still not clear to me. Neither did I believe in the non-violent way which might make me walk on my knees with the folded hands and open eyes upward. Gandhiji's *satyagraha* had a mass-appeal but that, too, has lost much of its force.

The democratic process, though long drawn-out and full of perplexes, is still my cup of tea.

Even so these inthings are tormenting my mind much as long before, but I have decided not to budge an inch from my commitment to the revolution of character to usher in the socialistic love.

All such mental torments disturbed my study. I had given word to my father that I would do well in the exam. So it was an unpleasant time for me, having little response from my within.

Before I did M.A. there occurred the Great Calcutta Killing. Communities were on a murderous spree, out to destroy the bond of brotherhood and human oneness. As a university student I could not stay behind and joined hands to organise peace missions in the riot-torn areas of the cursed city.

Responding to the call by Gandhiji I braved the weather and marched hand-in-hand from Beleghata to Chitpur via Rajabazar. Batchmate Tapan Piplai was with me, walking in silent peace. All the way divine blessings showered on us from pavements and rooftops, when, all of a sudden, while we were negotiating the Burrabazar area, some fanatics armed with swords and choppers attacked us, snapping the knot of peace and injuring many.

The Great Killing led to the Great Divide.

Our motherland was partitioned.

Bengal split, so did Punjab.

Where was the divine hand to stall the partition? The Indians worshipped the sub-continent as their dear motherland, an unearthly idea born of the godly thinking of the nation as a mother, but we parted ways in the bog of sly politicking and patitioned it like a dire slaughter house butcher without having little regard for its hoary cultural identity.

The tradition-bound spiritual bliss was missing while we let the knife cut into the core of Indian ethos. Where even were those pillars of the borrowed ideas we thrived on for decades? The dialectics, the materialism, and the socialism – all were gone with the wind!

My old notional, conceptual, values got hurt. My all arguments with all the socialistic do-gooders fell flat. Mistaken was I, so very much. I failed to make them understand that communalism would be too suicidal to be undone in years to come.

Our sweet motherland would be the haunting ground of the partition ghost. So it is.

The morning after the freedom at midnight was so confusing that our progressive ideologues did not at first accept the fait accompli and thought it was a fake independence.

Besides, most of us could not rise above inanity to measure the national perspectives in the new light, since we had been immersed in borrowed platitudes, since we just ignored the individual aptitudes in mankind, since our mental faculty had got incorrigibly stunted.

Clearly do I remember our village was spared the knife on the midnight of freedom. Its fate remained undecided in the Radcliffe Award. Days later, the Bagge Award came and Charghat stayed with India.

But those were the days of brutal uncertainty. Agony and anxiety pervaded all our minds, the minority Hindus thinking in hushed silence they would be left untouched while our majority Muslims harboured the idea of flying the Pakistani flag.

Hearbeats grew, we felt nervous as the day of decision advanced. The only relief was the 15th August of 1947 would not be the doomsday, for the Bagge Award would come afterwards. Still we did not take chances.

On the morning of August 15, we went on with our own independence celebration plans, even if we had reports the other community people were up to hatching their eggs. Their armed preparedness alarmed us, sending chill down our spines. We were a bit perplexed knowing little about what to do in maintaining peace and harmony. Yet the work on the day's programme of building arches draped in Tricolours and setting up the dais and mikes for a grand-scale meeting went on.

The meeting had been arranged with the idea of taking a decision on our future line of action whatever the Award. But nervousness pervaded the ground, all working with bated breath.

Our club members and the villagefolks had already gathered at the meeting ground under a big mango tree. It was three in the afternoon when the rival people started flowing in, mostly armed and raising the *larkey lenge* slogan that rent the sky and our hearts.

But there was total lull, possibly before the storm. All were standing in attention, and the silence queerly increased our heartbeats.

It was a wonder divinity that suddenly dawned on me and I shouted *Allah ho Akbar* thrice follwed by *Vandemataram* also thrice. Initially, there was a bit confusion but then went up the echoes just in order.

Wisdom prevailed, the finale symbolised by unity, all embracing one another. The meeting was hrriedly held with union board president Esahuq Akunji in the chair which passed a resolution that said, 'Come what may, we will live together'. The resolution had been drafted under the care of a club elder Hemendranath Banerjee.

The atomosphere changed, virtully eased, and sweet fellow-feeling, touched by emotional togetherness, spread through the darkening wood under the dusky sky. The Muslims offered *namaz* and the Hindus prayers. The pledge of unity rose from our divinity within, and never was the pledge given a bloody go-by.

The Bagge Award favoured the village in remaining within the Indian Union, yet seldom in subsequent years was there a strife.

A good friend of mine Rousan Ali of the neighbouring village Deora came to me one day. He was in tears. What was the matter? He told me sobbingly his family had decided to shift to East Pakistan (now Bangladesh). A settlement of property exchange had already been reached with a family from across the border.

'Don't worry. We'll remain friends as ever. We can't part ways,' I just could tell him. I did not know if that had given me any comfort.

Rousan left India never to return. He was of my age. What had happened to him I do not know till now.

Incidentally, Rousan's family will ever be remembered for donating their land where our present school Charghat Milan Mandir Vidyapith stands.

Down memory lane I went, and I recollect how my old father, then still alive, did react to the geo-political divide. The guillotine cut the nation into two, for which Khulna went into the other side of the border. Satkhira was snatched away. Our in-laws lived there. My father was sad, with agony and anguish writ large on his wrinkled face. No divine grace for the old man!

The unkind knife that could behead a culture with the twinkle of an eye brought in a swift change in the physiognomy of our village. The atmosphere changed; the character changed; and the population ratio at the daybreak turned into fifty-fifty.

And the social fabric lost its age-old texture.

The divinity within me was ruthless, making the turning point in my life different from the one that was politics-based social work to that of family compulsion, not a U-turn though.

5

POLITICAL SWING

Early fifties, at the dawn of 1952, my family funds were a compulsive factor in taking more than a half round to enter the world of journalism as a profession.

My career in communication began as an apprentice sub-editor in the news department of the *Hindusthan Standard*, then an English daily of the *Ananda Bazar* Group in Kolkata. The newspaper office was at Burman Street near Burrabazar. Later, it shifted to its own building at Sooterkin Street (now Prafulla Sarkar Street) near Esplanade.

It was a hard decision for me to change the course of life from law to information. But my early marriage to Usha and family commitments all made me go in for earning our livelihood. I understood my career-building in the legal profession would consume so much time that I could not afford.

Already I had my daughter Tanima My son Saumya would see the light soon. The decision was taken in haste. What else could I do? It seemed a wild expectation for the divinity within to manifest itself soon.

My father was annoyed. I sought his forgiveness. He was adamant. But, fortunately, after a month of dry apprenticeship, the office entered my name in the pay register.

Silently did I work on the news desk, keeping my eyes and ears open, since there was hardly anyone to teach me editing mechanics.

But my mind got disturbed with thoughts about my father and family all staying behind at village home. My father could never compromise with my journalistic career and my club companions accepted me no more as a living force in social life.

Truly, the initial years of my new life-turn were sort of a hybernation period, a real holiday in political polemics and social petty-fogging. But I had no intention of going into oblivion. I preferred to go in for soft-pedalling in daily tumults.

Was it a stoic quietitude? No, not at all. Only did I keep safe distance from activism in politics although my philanthropic work continued, a little abated, with divinity within putting a brake short of morbidity. Mine became a closed-circuit performance, limited to the school-library-theatre work.

What would usually come to my mind was the restless time ranging from 1949 to 1951. Almost everything was unsettled, without any positive objectives in view, and I was not earning then a paisa.

Moreover, I suffered a jail term in 1949 when the railway strike was stillborn. The Central Jail at Dum Dum was my home for months then.

Arrested at Sealdah station while I was trying to board a late-evening train bound for Bongaon early March that year, I was held and whisked away to a police post on the platform and made to sit down there for hours before some cruel searching eyes. Questions were hurled at me wildly that hurt me. Finding me a damp squib an Anglo-Indian sergeant jumped up and rushed forward to me with a baton in his hand. He struck my left little finger. Fractured, the pain in the finger was severe. Soon a senior Intelligence Branch officer waved his hand and restrained him from beating me blue. The officer came to me and soothingly said, 'It'll be all right'.

My carry-bag had alrealy been searched. Leaflets about the role of students in the railway strike were seized.

The IB officer asked me why I was carrying them. I smiled and answered, 'They were meant for distribution among students'.

'But these are political leaflets nothing to do with students! Am I right?'

'Yes, you are. But the students are not interested in knowing about the politics behind the strike. They want to know the proper perspective and get enlightened. Am I wrong?'

The questioner relented.

Past midnight I was sent to the GRP lock-up. I was hungry, but there was no food. Most probably, this amounted to being the divine punishment. Good heavens!

Inside the lock-up I found some persons sleeping, scattered, their faces covered. I sat alone in a corner of the room, half-dark and stinky.

Suddenly a thought flashed through my mind—perhaps by this time my residence had been raided by the police, who might have got the information about it from the scrappy diary I had kept in my bag. Would they harass my father and brother?

Next morning, amidst the slumberous din of the station platforms, I got a cup of steaming tea from a policeman. Was it godsend? Never mind, the tea was inebriating.

The cup was still not empty when an IB officer, not the one I had met last night, appeared before me and brought a chair to sit on. But finding me I was sitting on the dirty floor of the lock-up, he got up, took his chair and asked me to follow him. I was trembling, but wonder-struck as I was, I was offered a seat around a table. As I sat, I felt much relieved. Now, I was sitting with my back to the chair, not to the wall. Yet I could not stop dozing, my face desolate and hungry.

My ordeal started, and no divine grace. The clock struck nine and entered three or four other IB and CID officers and sat encircling me to begin their searching grill. No mercy for my discomfiture from my nightlong hunger—my backache and swoon, and exhaustion!

Countless queries and railleries they hurled at me. And the way they were asking about my activities immediately alerted me that they had taken away some valuable books and even pictures.

It was not a question-answer session, but a mad gruelling trial for some imaginary offences that I had not committed.

Q. Why are you studying politics?

A. I am dong M.A. in economics. Politics is a part of the subject.

Q. Is Grammar of Politics your text-book?

A. Yes, the book is in my syllabus. Harold Laski is the author. There is another book by Laski—An Introduction to Politics, also a text-book.

Q. All in your course?

A. Yes.

They stopped for a moment, possibly to get a breather. Suddenly then, they burst out : Are you conversant with socialism? Is that also a subject of your study?

Calmly did I answer : Yes, that is also a subject. I have to study it for marks.

Unrelenting they asked : What is its difference from communism?

I dared say : You seem to be interested in having an academic discussion with me. If you have time, I can make you understand it all. That will surely sharpen my memory.

They were silent. I said : Several questions on socialism and communism come in the M.A. exam and one has to answer as many of them.

I did not know why they gave up questioning me further. It was well past mid-day. There was no food. I remained hungry. They departed when some other policemen came and took over. I was made to walk to the magistrate's court at Sealdah. In the courtroom I was made to enter into an enclosure. The magistrate, without looking at me, went through police papers and sent me to jail custody.

From Sealdah to Dum Dum it was a long journey. At the gate of the Central Jail I got down from the prison van. Others, too, came down; probably, they were jail-birds.

I was looking scraggy, just a lump fighting hard to stand erect. Totteringly, I went in. The counting of heads began. Just then I dropped down with a thud. I was not unconscious but dazed, and I felt someone was holding me tight. 'Stand up', he whispered. I got up. He held me dearly. I recognised him. He was an old friend of mine who had been in the jail much earlier. He whispered again to me, 'Don't fall. Stand up. I'm holding you.' He was Mukul, my good friend Mukul Chakraborty.

'Ignore the head counting. That's an old British practice to which these jail people are still holding on. Come on. Sit in this verandah. Comfortably. I'm with you,' Mukul said to me a bit aloud, and angrily. The jail warden who had heard it did not mind it.

Mukul told me, 'Why are you so weak?'

'I didn't have anything to eat since last night. And all the time I had been kept awake. They were so rude, asking me all silly questions.'

'Did you answer them?'

'Only academically,' I smiled. 'They seemed to be interested in Laski.'

To my amazement, I found I was not alone in the jail. Several of my student friends had earlier been put inside. Even I found some Communist Party leaders talking shop inside the compound in front of their cells.

It was almost dark before I was taken to a big hall where I could get a blanket to spread on the floor to lie down. I did not wait. Stretching me with my hands pulled upwards I got the desired relief. My eyes closed when someone called me to get up and take my food. I got up. But was it food? I took a bite and left it there untouched. One of my hallmates gave me two biscuits, wherefrom I did not know. I munched them, ah! And then I drank a glass of water fully and fell down sleepy.

The whole night I slept well. I could not even dream of the divine bliss, if at all. Was it there? I was so tired that I did not get the right energy to fathom it within my depth.

A division three undertrial prisoner I was, never understanding why I had not been given classification as the division one prisoner despite my having the required educational qualification. I took courage and one day, when I was taken to the Sealdah court for hearing, I told bluntly the magistrate about my story. I argued convincingly my case for classification. The divinity within was aroused. My pleading did not go in vain. The magistrate for the first time looked at me. Wonder-struck, he asked me to write an application at once stating clearly my case. Surprisingly, a sheet of paper and a pen were handed to me. By whom I did not see. I wrote down my points and submitted the application to the magistrate, who took a glance at it and readily granted my prayer.

A little flutter arose in the courtroom, but the magistrate's angry face called everybody to order.

Soon afterwards I was brought to an adjacent room in the court house where I found a police officer was fuming with rage. I got him—he was angry.

And in the prison van, during my return trip to the jail, I got the respect due to an upgraded undertrial; I was offered a seat by the driver.

Book-reading, gossiping, speech-making and singing were my forte in the jail, but one day, surprisingly, veteran communist leader Satish Pakrashi invited me to play badminton with him. And, surprisingly again, he was such a good hand that I could not outplay him; rather, I surrendered to the 'grandmaster'.

Another day, I did not know why, Muzaffar Ahmed, the father-figure in the Indian communist movement, called on me and conversed with me for hours on topics of the time. Possibly, he knew I had an independent line of thinking, and this tete-a-tete might have pleased him. Good analyst Jolly M. Kaul and poet Subhash Mukhopadhyay befriended me with their mundane outlook.

But not all the days are blissfully sunny; sometimes people are in for rainy times.

Suddenly one day, there cropped up an unseemly outbrurst of anger while protesting against certain ugly misbehaviour of jail officials. We went on fast unto death. Negotiations started and after eighteen days the hunger-strike ended.

But soon began another round through some misunderstanding which continued for twelve days.

Even after one-month-long fast in two rounds we were feeling ill at ease with the jail management. As we smelt a rat in its attitude, we decided to disobey the jail command. The rule is the prisoners who walk around in the afternoon will have to enter their cells or halls at sunset. But one day we did not do as per the rule and remained outside on the road that divided the wings.

Scattered in groups, some sitting and some standing, we confronted a posse of armed policemen. Silence dawned, our cheeks hardened, the faces looked grim, and the eyes were gleamy. Carefully we noticed the movement of guards. Then the high gates were closed, the loudspeakers blared warnings, and the hoots and boots hit the grisly air.

And there were sudden bursts of gunfire.

Bullets flew over our heads. Several protesters ducked and escaped death. We the two friends, Mukul and myself, were standing utterly benumbed. A bullet straightway hit Mukul below the belt, blood gushing out profusely from his belly; he fell down and died in writhing pain. 'Sourin, lie down,' yelled Muzaffar Ahmed. I ducked and hastily lay prostrate. The bullet aimed at me missed the target and flew over my back. The divine bliss did not come from within but through famous Kakababu.

Well past midnight we went in, except Mukul, who lay down out in the open, the mist covering his body with white haze, and the blood underneath tinting the road red. I took the last look at him and gave him a mournful salute.

When the fast was on, one day a batch of guards, one of them an old man, came to our room aided by force-feeding equipment.

The old policeman was the havildar, in charge of the group who had come to nasal-feed me and others. I was lying on the bed spread on a cot that had been provided for me after I got the division one on the strength of the court order. The man, his white moustache flowing across his swollen cheeks, bent over me pleading with me that I did not move. But I resisted at first, and then resigned. Our seniors had advised us to offer moral resistance. I felt weak.

A day or two after this nasal feeding, the day of hearing of my case came, and I was taken on a stretcher to the prison van for the onward journey to Sealdah.

To my surpirise, I saw the old havildar was coming along with me by the stretcher. Looking at him I smiled but I could not hold my tears. On the force-feeding day, too, tears rolled down my cheeks and I clearly remembered the old man was holding out his hanky to wipe my tears off. He said then, 'Do you feel hurt?' I felt hurt, really, but even if I had a tough posture I could not keep my tears in check. And as he was wiping my tears from my cheeks, I felt astonished at this gesture as well. I then looked at him. He told me whisperingly, 'I do have a boy like you. Don't get nervous.'

Just I could raise my head lying on the stretcher to see the old man disappear after closing the door of the prison van. Lowering my head I shut my eyes.

Staggeringly, I appeared before the magistrate, who took no time to grant me an unconditional bail. My lawyers, the seniormost among them being my village uncle living nextdoor, came to me. One junior lawyer whispered into my ears, 'The police may re-arrest you, we suspect, for keeping you under detention without trial.'

My father and brother, who were present at the court, appeared concerned.

The lawyer told me, 'Better you should not move out now. Relax, and you're too weak. The police might be waiting at the gate.

My lawyer-uncle held a hurried discussion with my father and his colleagues. He advised change of my dress for a comouflage. My brother went home to bring a new set for me. In the meanwhile, I was shifted to a room upstairs and kept confined.

Within an hour or so the brother returned with the new set. I underwent a sartorial change.

Both my father and brother had by then left. So had the lawyers. I was alone in the room, beside a half-shut window, waiting for a signal from the lawyer. I felt a bit nervous. Could I make it?

Ultimately, holding my hanky to my nose and keeping alert though with false-step, I made it and stealthily slipped out of the gate. Out on the road I found a tramcar going south. I jumped into it but fell outside. I was too weak. And there arose shrieks all over. However, undaunted, I got up. There was no car moving on the track. My body was shaken. Just then I saw another streetcar on the other track going north. I could manage to get in, prespiring. Near Rajabazar I got a seat. At Fariapukur stop I got down from the car and somehow walked up to the Deshbandhu Park where a near relation of mine resided. It was early afternoon. I took rest and felt better.

My 'didi', as I still called her so even if she was my in-law, gave some food and while eating I narrated the entire story to her and said, 'Don't worry, I'll soon leave the place for Bowbazar where I live.' 'Didi' Anila Chatterji was silent.

'The police?' said my 'didi'.

'My feeling is they'll keep watch on me, but they won't arrest me now. Was it really so easy to give them the slip at the court gate?

'But you are so weak.'

'Satin will get me admitted to his hospital. He's the house staff there.'

It so happened. I was removed to hospital for malnutrition. The doctor asked me about my fast. 'And will the police take you back to jail again?'

'That I don't know.'

I did not know either if the police had already tracked me to the hospital. But they might have had the information that I was in bed.

A little better in health, I came back home at Bowbazar. Bad luck, I could not take rest for long. Some unfamiliar faces soon started hanging around our residence. My father had some uneasy feelings; my brother, too, had.

One evening I left home and via Manihari Ghat I arrived at friend Sachin Biswas's house at Kishanganj, away in Bihar.

My friend and his relations had a little surprise at seeing me without notice and I had an undisturbed time for some days. Sachin introduced me to a local literary group where one evening I sang Rabindra Sangeet though with much effort. I was too weak to give a good rendering, yet I was happy.

But, one night, Sachin came home sad and broody. I was wondering what had happened. He said, 'Just now I'm coming from the thana where the OC told me very curtly that Sourin Babu is a dangerous political element. Please don't give him shelter. I've orders for his immediate deportation.'

Sachin looked at me. I told him not to worry. 'I won't embarrass you. Buy me a train ticket for Kolkata. I'll go.'

What then, he queried.

Come what may, I just answered.

Next afternoon I got into a train bound for Manihari Ghat via Katihar. My plan was I would board a ferry at Manihari Ghat to cross the Ganga and land at Sakrigali Ghat to board a standing bogey for going to Sahebganj where may bogey would be linked to a night train bound for Howrah.

At Kishanganj station, while the train was waiting at the platform for signal, I noticed two constables entered the same compartment as mine and sat on the bench facing me.

The train left the station. My friend remained standing, waving his hand in despair, his look vacant, and I was in tears as I responded to him as long as he could be seen. No divine grace, then!

On the sandy bank of the Ganga the train halted. A kind of makeshift station it was. I got down, the bag in my hand. The sacred river caught my awful eyes. Its muddy brownish waters, swelling. swirling and splashing, were an eyeful of fury. The steamer would have to cut across the tremendous flow downstream. I boarded it along with others, but where were the policemen who had been tracking me so long? I looked around but found them nowhere.

The steamer was moving through foaming waves. In a few moments it reached the other shore. Berthed at an improvised jetty, its crew opened the exit gate to let the passengers get down on the soaked sand.

Walking on the vast sandy bank to reach the waiting coach far away was an exercise. Fast did I move into a compartment and spread a *chaddar* on the upper bunk. Without losing time I lay down straight and went into deep slumber.

I slept the whole night. I did not know when the bogey had been linked to the Howrah-bound train at Sahebganj. The din and noise at Howrah next morning awakened me.

Virtually a total broke I returned home. My father enquired about my health. 'You look so run-down.'

'Nothing like that, but I'm too hungry'.

Some time afterwards I peeped through a window to see if I was still being watched but I did not find any unfamiliar face out in the street.

Thoughts flashed my mind : It's divine grace, I'm no longer wanted by the police!

Once, a few days later, I visited Bongaon to speak at a rally by students who had been agitating against fee increase. It was an academic issue, but the local administration lost no time in giving it a political hue. The rally was held in the magistrate's compound.

The rally over, students dispersed peacefully, but I left the town in a huff as I feared arrest. At a place, miles away from the town thana, I spent hours until dawn and then hurried to a nearby station to catch an early morning train. I had bought a ticket for Kolkata but got down at a midway station.

In the house of my cousin sister at Gobardanga I took shelter for noontime meal. Then early in the evening the same day I left for Charghat. After a long detour I reached home at dead of night.

My father was startled to see me at the doorstep. He said, 'How're you?'

I comforted him by saying 'O.K. Don't worry. You?'

He did not answer me but only said the Swarupnagar thana police one day came to our house and ransacked all rooms.

'Why?'

'They said they had information that arms and bombs were stored in a hideout inside.'

'Did they get any?'

'No.'

'Then?'

'All the household earthenwares, brassmetal articles and other artefacts were damaged, broken and thrown away.'

Before dawn I left my village home. My father was standing at the door, as usual, blessing me with his right palm on my head. I touched his feet and did not turn back to see his tearful face again.

I did not see my brother at home. He was away in the city on errands. My cousin sister, who used to look after my father, was inside the house, calm and glum.

Bad luck, I had nowhere to go. To Kolkata? No, not after the Bongaon movement. And the police knew my city address. I went underground. Away in Naihati I got a shelter, not temporarily, but soon I got tired of hiding for so long. I was at my wit's end.

Ultimately, I shifted to my city residence. My brother stayed there at that time. He was surprised to see me as if out of nowhere.

'Are you well?'

'Yes.'

'Cops here, following you?'

'No. They're away.'

'What then has happened? Have you changed the line?'

'That I don't know, but what is certain is I don't want to be a cadre nor a leader in any party. The party line is not my forte.'

'What will you do?'

'I want to do social service.'

'Ah! I smell a rat. There, too, politics......'

'I know it. Too well. But I won't do any party politics: That kind of thing is an aversion, and I die to the world.'

My brother stopped talking; he just looked at me in wonder. Probably, he might be thinking about my volte face. I guessed it and said, 'Don't think I'm fleeing away, but the truth is politics is not the natural bent of mine.'

Still then, as it was the election time in our country, and that was the first general election in independent India, I took part in campaigning for a progressive candidate of great repute, as he was personally known to me. And he won.

For some time then I had been in journalism, but my father's angst against my abjuring law for ever remained unabated, as a holdover of his resentment at my opting for pen and not wig.

One day he scolded me mercilessly. He said, 'Now you're married, yet you don't seem to be serious, doing nothing substantially for the family, still an unceremonious parasite.'

I got it all in the neck. Along with Usha I left home and headed for Purnea where friend Sachin was then posted as a government employee. Oddly, this time I did not have the blessings of my father which had been the usual thing in my all past pursuits.

And divinity within remained this time strangely indifferent.

Misfortune and misery came all at a time. It was too difficult for Sachin to take the load. I did appreciate his trying time, but I was helpless.

Soon was born my son Saumya, a brother to my little daughter Tanima. My mother-in-law, along with my brother-in-law Pannalal Mukherjee, hurried to Purnea to see things out there. My 'dada' returned with unwholesome stories about their bad time. I took leave of absence from my office which I had joined a few days earlier and went to Purnea to bring back Usha and two children.

My father, in the meantime, fell ill and wanted to see Usha and children. I took them home. Seeing them, and particularly my son, he smiled.

And then I had the divine bliss. My brother, who had married by then and had a son, hurried home from Burdwan, then his place of practice.

Gradually, I became a slowcoach in politics. Not a deserter, though. But, grown up in age, I found I was a bit misfit even in student politics, for which I opted out of the known orbit, neither joining the party bandwagon.

And my constant brooding over what was to be done that would fit in well with sitruations goaded me into thinking that the Indian soil was not ripe for living on borrowed dogmas which seemed to be too rigid to get adjusted with the parliamentary democracy we were then trying out.

Besides, political rigidity did not tally with the individualistic human element ingrained in the socialistic human overture to democracy being constantly disturbed by the bureaucratic overlordship born of regimented privileges.

Why should socialist-modellers, in their urge for acquisitive regimentation, give up the element of individualistic truth I did not understand. As I got it, class struggle did not mean mass uprising for enthroning the rule of the elite. The dictatorship could not degenerate into an elitist thumb-rule. A new privileged class grew up replacing the old one, opposed to what the Marxists had thought of and also to that of the Vedantic ideal of oneness.

And there was no point in pursuing the international polemics on the home front, the one which was different from the alien one. International communism would be an exercise in utopian ideal, never to bring the vast world under one roof with so many interests vying with one another to get the upperhand in political universalism. My firm protest was against subordination to foreign models; my fault was I harped on the theme of evolving a pragmatic domestic strategy to develop the root, the result also of my divine thinking.

We did not believe in inner-contradictions in the socialistic system, but our belief got a severe jolt during the Sino-Indian border conflict. India was then following the socialistic pattern as modelled by Pandit Jawaharlal Nehru while China proclaimed communism. Still the two countries clashed. Both the Soviet Union and China took to the communist path of development, yet they were involved in umcompromising polemics that finally led to the global split. Some of the Soviet Bloc countries went back to square one and market economy took over, excepting China which opted for a modified version of twin opposite economies.

The Gorbachev regime in the Soviet Union succeeded in ending the cold war with the United States and bringing in the open-window political phenomenon, but failed in making glasnost and perestroika a resounding success. Yeltsin took over and went in for swift 'balkanization' of the Soviets to take Russia into the limelight but failed in the quick switch to benevolent market economy. Its efforts at solving the Chechnia and distant Bosnia problems created only hullabaloo.

North Korea, Vietnam and Cuba were till then holding the fort though with increased fear and decreased vigour.

Euro-communism, a deviant socialist model that had craned its neck in the European belt and was experimenting with coalition governments in different countries, did not fall through but failed to make a mark in revolutionising the 'socionomy'.

And various communist parties started disintegrating into rivals, some formidable, some feeble, all in disarray though putting up brave faces and trying to dispel disenchantments.

While in Britain, in 1966, as a Thomson Foundation scholar doing higher editorial studies, I chanced upon some old friends of mine then living there for livelihood and took a fund-raising move for fighting general elections far away in India. It culminated as a utopian gym and when I was back home I found the socialist movement had been disjointed beyond repair.

I was not a partyman, yet I felt sad at the debacle of a new experiment with improving the lot of the world have-nots. And in India the movement was split down the middle, the twin brothers now at loggerheads.

Divinity seemed to have betrayed me. I looked for the bliss, for its manifestation as a soothing balm, but the result was zero. Two poles remained asunder in one globe. Was it not an irony? All my pleadings with the Indian practitioners of politics failed. They did not heed me for a planned socialistic take-off from the soil of the country. So vast a land that India is, yet for the take-off we had to use the runway in Moscow or in Beijing.

One afternoon I arrived at Maslandpur to catch a Sealdah-bound train. I was in a hurry as I was late, but the train left the station without me. I was standing on the platform, dazed. I would have to do night duty but now how could I do it? Suddenly I noticed a bus crossing the level crossing. Certainly, it was going to Habra, a station away. I ran and got into it.

On reaching Habra I came to learn a train was about to leave for Sealdah. Again I was running but was this time held up by some friends busy jostling nearby. Holding me tightly they virtually dragged me to the first floor of a shop which was their party office.

'Why are you doing it so? I have nothing to do with any party or its politics.'

'We know that, *dada*. We have no other alternative. We are sorry. We all are in utter confusion. We want to talk to you for our enlightenment. And we know you will be the right person to guide us.'

'But I am not a committed cadre as you are. You know I have always been free-minded without having any berth anywhere.'

'Please Sourinda, tell us what we will do.'

'I can, but it will be my own opinion.'

'We just want to hear you.'

It was a big hall, filled to capacity. 'Go the Indian way'– was my first sentence. And soon there was hushed silence. And then I harped on the same tune as I had been doing so long. But what would be the right way I was not sure about. Yet I said, 'It must be the way the Indian conditions would determine. I am still in search of it. I am as much confused as you are.'

Then I tried to explain why the revolution had degenerated into polemics and why the progressive movement was splitting into sects. The permanent revolution theory had been illusory while the exercise in socialism in one country had lost its efficacy because of diehard bureaucracy. Proletarian authoritarianism, for lack of requisite education, and cultural revolution, for fear of losing heads, had only led to the leftwing infantile disorder.

Then?

Our Indian brethren were losing ground for they just ignored their country's objective conditions, for which, I was afraid, they might become satellites to national or regional parties. And the party divide was becoming wide and uncompromising.

I told the audience, in an emphatic voice : What's polemics to us? How does it affect us? Are our conditions same as theirs? Will we do what they do?

No uproar, a queer silence all over, all looking at me dazed and fazed.

'It's too difficult for us to bridge the gulf in the world arena. We've been sadly used to living on imported motivations. Am I wrong if I say this has been going on since the days of Renaissance? Moguls did not influence our thinking much, but the English wave virtually swept us away. Now we're free from foreign yoke; we must start thinking anew, and that should be the Indian way, conditioned by the smell of the country's own self.'

There was a pause; I was taking a breather. Then again I burst out, 'Don't be carried away by alien emotions. Go your way, and you decide which way you'll go. Please don't forget your root is in this country, not elsewhere.'

The one sorry thing I had noticed before I started talking to the audience that the dividing line was well defined, and I was talking hardly any sense to the divided house. Brain-washing was almost complete!

And I felt I was woefully alienated. And all my heuristic heroics were on a dream never come true.

Then I just ran out of the apparently mum crowd for a train to office.

Under a cloudless sky one day I was standing still on a village path wondering how would I reform my walk of life. Alone! Suddenly tree leaves stirred; squirrels jumped from one branch to another; sun-bathed birds sat quietly on twigs; cattle-heads were munching grass or chewing the cud; and rural folks were wending their ways through forest tracks. Numbed as I was, I did not notice that a hissing snake had already come near me with its fang spread. It scared me and I took a nervous leap aside. Blessings showered on me. From where, I did not know. But I saw the snake disappear into bushes.

Was it divinity within that had spared my life? I had no answer, but I had been chilled to the bone. I got back life on my mother earth. And did it mean I hold on to ground? As I was advising my Habra friends to do?

6

JOURNALISTIC PURSUIT

The journalistic career that I chose for my walk of life made me a real down-to-earth man and in all seriousness did I never fail to keep my ears and eyes open for seeing things around and getting the knowledge of men and matters in their right perspectives. This would ever satisfy my never-ending yearning for information, and I thought if I was satisfied with its proper dissemination the readers for whom I worked would also have the same feeling.

Satisfying everybody's palate is a difficult task, I knew it. And that might mean pleasing none. Still I never shied away from my information work.

As a communicator I cannot keep anybody in dark. To achieve this end I worked from start till finish of the newspaper publication.

The bliss of sunshine comes after the bane of darkness and I tried to follow the rule with honesty and integrity. The sunny possibility always emboldended me to take the plunge into the profession learning the tricks of the art of attraction through wordcare and news-treatment.

Just a divine onlooker I was not; my search within made me a participative seer of facts that mattered in news development. All tidings, topical or futuristic, I would get by heart, for intellectual update, by looking over the shoulders of other colleagues, never by going by the book. And never did I want to remain glued to rigid doctrinaire approaches to the dynamics of journalism. In printing technology, too, I tried to be adept.

When I succeeded in making the grade as a professional journalist, my editor Sudhansukumar Basu was all praise for me. Blessings again!

Earlier, journalists did not have any protective shield. They were at the mercy of their employers, but later, after a few years of independence, the law came, to be called the Working Journalists Act, in short, that gave the employees a status and recognition, a total turnaround in life-style. These pen-people became well paid, some highbrowed.

Our national newspapers, as a legacy of the olden era of dependence, had the proclivity of overplaying the speeches and movements of leaders. News did not have the play according to merit. Managements focussed mainly on the liberation struggle while readers did not mind reading undue presentations.

But perspectives changed with the birth of freedom when readers started asking for worthwhile news and play and managements began arguing for more space allotments for advertisements. Eyes were riveted towards increased space and paper sales. Naturally, news-doers paid their attention to meeting the needs of the time.

Oldtimers in the profession were often hardliners not easily giving in, but new-comers like me went in for a change in the stereotyped outlook, everytime fighting the old unprofessional love.

The change of guard was not smooth. Trimming speeches to bare bones and cutting leaders to sizes met with resistance, but we did not relent, and ultimately Operation Space was a success. A wonder era of removing extra fat from stories written in longish jargons and paraphrases began, with a bang. Merit-play became the watchword.

A viable face-lift appeared in my paper *Hindusthan Standard* and seen off were ill planning and dumping.

My earlier political sojourns helped me to develop democratic, if progressive, postures, making me amenable to one and all whatever their personal likes and dislikes. My participative role, enriched by the bliss of divinity within, gave me the required back-up reward.

And my working with high-ups from the International Press Institute, Zurich, acted as a booster.

Much benefit I derived from the refresher course run by the Press Institute of India, Delhi. It was in 1963. And three years later in 1966, I went to Cardiff, in Britain, as a Thomson Foundation scholar for making higher editorial studies.

Several of the national and provincial newspapers I visited in Britain, and at Fleet Street in London my meeting editors and other newsmen was very rewarding. And the tug-of-war between serious and popular dailies gave enough of opportunities to me to gather newer ideas of newspaper making. In London most big dailies I visited which included *The Times*, *Daily Express*, *The Daily Telegraph* and *Daily Mail*, besides the tabloids like *Daily Mirror* and *The Sun*. At Edinburg I had the chance to go round the offices of *The Scotsman*. But at Cardiff the *Western Mail* was our daily rendezvous. Modern technologies were then gradually taking over, though computerization was still not widely known.

It was a pleasure to meet tophat newsman Harold Evans, who was then the managing editor of *Sunday Times*. Later, he took over as editor of the paper because its editor Dennis Hamilton had joined *The Times* as its head.

One day I met Hamilton in his office in London and asked him if he had big plans to bring about any face-lift in the conservative paper. He smiled and said, '*The Times* is an institution.'

From London I had been on a short tour of West Germany (now it's Germany, after the fall of the Berlin wall). Lights all the way marked the trip to Koln from where I drove to Bad Gadesburg, a hilly and chilly town by the Rhine near Bonn, the then capital city. I put up at Hotel Inter Nationes.

At lunch one day in a Rhine-side cafe I had a chance meeting with indologist Dr. Fischer, who stayed in Kolkata once. He used to call me 'Rasgolla Babu' as I was a teetotaller. We enjoyed the noontime much. At Dusseldorf I met the news editor of a local daily newspaper. In response to my query about Ruhr he said the Germans were not raising coal from pits; instead they were importing it from abroad for it was cheaper than the Ruhr coal.

The visit to Hamburg was highly pleasant with river trips on the waves at the port. But the air travel to Berlin across East Germany was bumpy, the jet often losing the altitude, the pilot often asking us to pray to God, but finally the landing in Berlin was safe. I would admit I had too often delved deep within me to get the divine bliss.

Berlin was then to me a wonder city, the war-ravaged western part bubbling with new life and the eastern part still limping in ruins. West Berlin had the landmarks like the bombarded church, Brandenberg Gate and the Berlin Wall as the great divide with the East where I saw the Peace Statue and the green graveyard of Adolf Hitler.

The Berlin Wall then prevented the handshake.

A thought flashed through my mind : The Bengal Wall would remain a permanent divide!

It was late afternoon one day when I left Berlin for Frankfurt, for my onward journey to Paris. The jet I was flying in soon pierced clouds and flew past rainbows. Splended, naturally! I felt like touching the orange hue, but the aircraft window stood in between.

Down I came on the Maine, the river flowing by the airport at Frankfurt. The halt was short. Soon the jet left the runway and soared high to touch the stars above; it was sun-down then. The Orly airport in Paris looked like a fairy gateway to the beauty on earth. All the city over was flashed white with lights glowing. I came to the lounge and after initial hazards I won entry into the wonderland.

Putting up at a cheap Algerian hotel near the Notterdam church of the hunchback fame, I had a wash and some fast food, and then I was out in the street. Well past midnight I strolled. Paris did not sleep but by two or three in the morning I lolled on the hotel bed. I did not sleep either.

Early next morning, after a heavy breakfast, I went out and headed for the Eiffel Tower on the river Seine. It was another wonder, the steel frame tapering off to a tip touching the hazy morning sky, and later as the sky cleared, its conical shape appeared soaring high to kiss the cloud.

Half the height of the tower an elevator lifted me, the rest half being out of bounds for the public. While standing on the railed-off platform I had a grand view of the enchanting spectacle that is Paris.

And yonder a faint outline of the Notterdam church was visible but the Bastille was lost in the mist.

Down below the tower a broad street could be seen with cars in rows running at breakneck speed. The Parisians though swollen with winter outfits on, were walking fast. On the Seine cruising steamers or motorboats were all crowded, some afloat with poise.

Walking lazily along the boulevard I spotted the famous Arc-de-Triumph, sunlit and beaming, cars racing alongside on the sprawling wide road.

Crossing the road was an impossible job; I took the subway to go over to the other side. A little far away stood in silence the Invalids of the Nepolean Bonaparte fame, but just in front of me stood a wide open door to a building where Pablo Picasso's works of art were on show.

Mid-day. I was hungry. From a wayside cafe I bought sandwiches and coke. Thereafter I proceeded towards the Elysee Palace where de Gaulle was then living. With a bird's eye view from outside I remained pleased.

While I was roaming about in the gigantic office complex it started drizzling. Knowing from people where the Louvre was, I ran for it. Inside the famous museum in the French capital I found a big hall wet from dripping overcoats and there was hanging on the wall ever-smiling Monalisa, welcoming me in with her eyes fixed on me, seen from any angle. Really, the great painting by Leonardo de Vinci was eye-piercing. Many people thronged the hall end to end, as though in a trance.

Downstairs, in a room, stood Venus the beauty, but the exotic sculpture had a hand mangled.

All over the Louvre, sidewalls and underroofs, all decorated with murals and frescos, made me spell-bound. And divinity that had arisen from within me pervaded all around, a meaningful wonder, indeed. All great creations are divine. The art divine! Forever. And the manifestation in me often attained a sublime height which was beyond my comprehension. Was it a scientifically research-based result?

By a Metro train I reached the Notterdam church. Looking up I saw the big bell the hunchback had used to call up his ladylove. My neck was aching.

From a wayside trolley some fried chestnuts I bought and ate, the taste being that of our country's jackfruit seeds fried in ovens. My village suddenly came to my mind and I felt nostalgic.

The Bastille landmark was a distance away. I just walked down to it. History touched my heart. It was a fortress in Paris that served as a prison until its destruction on July 14, 1789, in the French Revolution. I thought I was walking into the history.

The sun was diving down into the western horizon. Hurrying to the hotel I packed up. Bag and baggage I soon left the hotel and took a taxi to reach the terminal for boarding the bus to the airport. At Orly I looked behind and caught a sight of the Eiffel Tower basking in the affection of neons.

The flight to London took off a little later and soon the love-city of the world was left behind. The plane soared and was airborne with the moon above shining half-baked.

After some time, scattered dots of light I could locate far below on the English Channel. Then they disappeared into darkness and I found the plane was circling over the starry city of London. The touchdown was smooth. Near the door out I spotted my friend waiting for me.

Hiring a cab at the terminal Dulu and myself soon arrived in North London where his uncle lived. Seeing a copy of the *Le Monde* (in Paris I had bought it for a look at it) the uncle jumped and grabbed it for reading. I thought he must be knowing the language French, which was Greek to me.

Of course, I had in the meantime surveyed the display of headlines without knowing their meanings. Now I got the opportunity to know them from the uncle. Dulu had been smiling at my innocence. Was it not a blissful simplicity, eh?

Earlier, in Berlin I had gone through a copy of the *Die Welt* just superficially, but the display appeared to me well-styled.

Contents of both the newspapers were not intelligible to me as I did not know the languages and the wordcare required for the right conveyance of information. Instant information, I meant.

On the table at Dulu's place I found two London newspapers, the broadsheet *Daily Mail* and the tabliod *Daily Mirror.* It surprised me to see the *Daily Mail* had made a departure from the traditional news display that would go right. The paper, instead, had placed the lead story in the central splash, the point of section of two diagonal lines resembling the multiplication sign, with the top left, in the primary optical area, running a horizontal spread. The pattern looked strange as most people were not used to reading the cross-section first. And the readers finally rejected this kind of odd departure from the normal optical movement. Finally, the daily reverted to the old style.

The *Daily Mirror,* however, did not upset its old frontpage-backpage equation, as I found it was putting equal emphasis on these two pages. Shouting headlines used to come in the twin pages because turning over from front to back pages was easy and effortless.

British newspapers went in for depth reporting and the digging was mainly intended to give the readers an insight into the fact. It was like going behind fact. All for truth.

News writing, too, had gone in for a change, from crude paraphrasing to analytical explaining. A part of depth report, indeed. Similarly, editorials were beginning with ends, explanations and exhortations following. While columnists preferred personalised impressions, feature-writers tried to get the right kick-off with interviews becoming more intimate and incisive. And more spaces were devoted to sports, business news and lighter asides.

Full of ideas I returned to my desk work in Kolkata but I did not open my cards all at a time. I kept up some of them in my sleeves for timely disclosure.

Newspapers in our country were still then tied to the hotmetal process. They were trying out newer technologies to catch up with the world trend dominated by software devices and cold processes. The new and the old were hemispheres apart. Internet and Intranet methods were not known then but today they are bynames dominating the scene in editing and printing. Computers were gaining ground when I retired in 1985, silently.

For about four years after my retirement I worked in two Bengali newspapers and one news weekly.

I had retired after my rich experiences as the news editor of the *Hindusthan Standard* and *Business Standard*, two English dailies of the city. And these experiences did greatly help me in producing the Bengali papers, though I did not get the chance to use the modern technology.

Divinity in this case has not blessed me. No wonder, then, the earthly handicaps have stood in the way of my getting the ticket for doing exercises within.

7

ACADEMIC ASSIGNMENT

Teaching became a challenging job of mine, as a part-timer, though. My principal avocation was journalism, and still I might take pride in doing the teaching job seriously making the mark in interacting with students comfortably well.

And this academic thrust got its grand take-off after my return from the educational trip to Britain where I made higher studies in editing newspapers as a Thomson Foundation scholar.

Even though I had done well in my M.A. exam I did not join the teaching line because my father Nagendranath opposed it by saying that he had to rot as a teacher for long thirty-six years. Though a maths prodigy, my father had to accept the work as a teacher at the instance of my grandmother. Father left his job in the Indian Museum to become an ill-paid educator, just to satisfy my grandma for looking after landed property in our village and around, because the teaching job would provide him with enough of time for monitoring the expanding interests.

Father was not happy with the new assignment but he did not go against the wishes of his mother. He was so obedient. But afterwards, as I grew up, I understood he was sore with this kind of docile life-style. He had little time to think of anything else than his landed property. And, besides, in performing what he had been assigned to do he did not have any substantive cooperation from his brother, my uncle Sailendranath.

Perhaps, my uncle thought whatever his elder brother did, would be satisfactory. Why should he interfere then? Or, maybe, he had little interest in estate building when money would be flowing in from other sources in the city. Over his indifference my father quarrelled with the uncle but to no purpose.

There was another kind of anguish in my father's humble mind. He did not get due recognition of his talent in mathematics. Once he told me he used to play sum-games with his friends like Jadav Chandra Chakrabarty and K.P. Basu, the former a wizard in arithmetic and the latter in algebra. What was disheartening was both of them, all good friends, had nowhere acknowledged their debt to my father.

And shamefully for me, I did not do well in maths in the Matriculation Examination, in 1941; so it was because I could not get his blessings nor the divine grace. And the aftermath of my educational life took a diversionary line when I developed a very keen interest in the upcoming and dynamic subject like economics, with politics as an appendage. Also did I do law but did not practise it for lack of luck and fund.

The financial stringency forced my brother, who was by then a good doctor, to leave the village. He joined the West Bengal Health Services and got his first posting in a village at Burdwan. I also started thinking of getting an employment, as the family ordeal was too heavy.

Which career would I prefer? Education was a taboo; law was too fanciful; and office-job was not to my liking. Any other job, then, that would come by?

I grabbed journalism.

My father died in 1961, paving the way for my taking up the teaching job of my choice. But my editor did not allow me to do so. I was then the deputy news editor of my newspaper and seriously working for a major breakthrough in news-catering. He, however, permitted me to join Calcutta University as a part-time faculty in the journalism department where he was the head as well as the dean. I was associated with the department for long twenty years at a stretch, virtually with full marks in interacting with students. My subject was first Making of a Journal – Paper 2, but later, after the revision of the syllabus, I taught Editing – Paper 4. All this gave me an immense scope for specialization in news editing.

While teaching cosmetic journalism in my classrooms I found the books authored by foreign writers did not exemplify situations in the Indian press. Practices of the newspapers overseas were generally, if liberally, incorporated in these books, and our students by and large grope in the dark to get at the perspectives behind such illustrations.

Not only did I face the problems in teaching in Calcutta University where the journalism course began primarily in M.A., since at the graduation level this discipline had not by then gained a common momentum of urge, but also at the Bhartiya Vidya Bhavan in the city where there was only the post-graduation journalism diploma course. As I was the co-ordinator faculty, I had to discuss the basics of communication which was unnecessarily time-consuming.

In both places, while I came over to discussing the cosmetics, much of my valuable time was lost, and uselessly for that matter.

So did I, along with other considerate fellow-men, fight hard to get journalism as a subject in the B.A. curriculum, honours or pass. Because that would largely facilitate the updating of teaching. Nowadays the picture is different. Journalism, both pass and honours, is taught as an undergraduate discipline.

But the poverty of relevant books prevailed, and to fill in the gap I myself, with the blessings from within standing by me, jumped upon the idea of writing text-books for college and university levels. And behind my efforts were the inspiring hands of my family – wife Usha, daughter Tanima and sons Saumya and Arya.

In all publications I took care in flooding them with indigenous practices and illustrations and diagrams, all combined to help students understand the art. My books written in English are *News Editing in Theory and Practice, Reporting Manual, Editing Manual* and *Journalism – An Overview*. Besides, my Bengali book is entitled *Samachar Sampadana.* And there is a Bengali translation of an English book.

I would not claim all my books are of high standard, but what has pleased me much is the editions have been prescribed as text-books by some institutions and well received by neo-profs and students. What else than such admiring words I merit? And admiration – can I say so gently? – is born when life is divine.

Among the books the *Samachar Sampadana* in Bengali is an update though principally related to Bengali journalism in the State of West Bengal made suitable for higher study. And the latest English edition *Journalism – An Overview* is an update of both print and broadcast networks, with explorative references to the Internet and Intranet highways.

Homework I would do well before I went to take a class. It is a dynamic subject I taught, a subject that is ever changing with the times keeping track of the changing technology. Editing techniques are forever related to printing technologies. A teacher having an experience in applied journalism must know about it, otherwise he will be driven to the backseat and his students will be denied information.

A teacher who always keeps to the right track is never a flop; rather, he oftentimes with his competence rises to a height which gives him a philosophical yet intellectual pleasure. And this competence is innate blessed by divinity.

Several thought-provoking articles I have written; several new ideas and ways I have spoken of. My piece *Hundreds of Memories, A Few Words* printed in the *Sangbadik* of Calcutta Journalists Club, of which I was once the president and a lifelong member, covered the transition from paraphrased speeches to analytical indepths.

The CU department once organised a journalism congress presided over by Press Council chairman A.N. Grover. 'Publish or Perish' was the theme article that was written by me and carried in the *The Journalist* duly published on the occasion. Aggressive journalism was the order of the day then and I hammered a point home which said : If we do not put across what we have to say boldly, we will perish.

In that article I argued we are living in a market of cut-throat competition and our contemporaries are ever on their toes to beat us in the run and will steal the thunder by taking what we will miss out of fear. So my advice was : Be aggressive. Bite, without malice. Remember bite is not spite.

I also wrote 'Press under Duress' in the journal, clarifying the numerous pressures under which we work. About this topic I also spoke at a seminar away in Ranchi, but quite strangely I stirred up the hornet's nest. I was sorry to say news delayed or even suppressed is news denied, and this kind of impropriety on the part of news-dishers put the journalists in duress.

'Reporting Chhotanagpur' was the theme of the Ranchi open-hall conference. The Press Club president there, Bisweswar Chatterjee, was in the chair. He asked me to say something about it. I was thinking about how I would begin my extempore speech. In my hand I had a souvenir published on the occasion. Unmindfully I just opened up a page wherein I found to my surprise an article on Barefoot Journalists written by the man in the chair himself. I immediately took the cue from it and lambasted take-it-easy correspondents for their addiction to conducted tours, lavish handouts and hot drinks. I said they prepared their own reports on such so-called made-to-order materials and it was a shame when they lazily sent out these for publication in newspapers.

Were they printable matters? 'Why don't you go barefoot to the remotest corners of the Chhotanagpur region for getting us worthwhile reports? Only then you can expect your reports will see the light'.

The hall was silent, the audience dumb. They were possibly thinking whatever they were sending out were mostly wastepaper words not worth coming in print. All bright sides did not make stories; where were the dark sides? The real picture of the Chhotanagpur area was not just a made-easy story. I thundered out and wanted the correspondents to go barefoot to the region, meet people, talk to them, and then write up your dispatches. Tutored and trained reports would seldom get columns.

At a South Calcutta Rotary Club function once I made a speech on Better Tomorrows in journalism in which I referred to the emerging writing methods and printing devices. Some printing shop high-ups came over to me and embraced me endearingly.

Were not all these divine dispensations?

Calcutta Journalists Club, years ago, held an assembly to felicitate me in appreciation of my services to journalism and in response to whatever had been said I only gave my juniors an advice – learn anew and stay on. I had to harp on the tune of switching to total computerization and global information.

High ethos and ethics always got good reception from my students. I use to tell them : Don't be a beggar or a pettyfogger in your profession. Be brave and get the due. Slave and servile journalism will kill your bold instinct as a communicator.

And, please, no sloppy writings which are born of shallow materials sold by news brokers! We are still amazed to find there are professionals who are prone to mirky pastures.

Journalism update, as my impulsive divine manifestation dictates, is the key to understanding the quick pace of developments in the information world, and if one has the necessary update one can comfortably be up-and-coming.

Fast-growing infotechs keep editors on their toes, news at finger-tips is now the keep; the inthing being competition one cannot forgo alert mind, open eye, sharp intelligence, keen ear and strong memory, all aided by electronics, computers, zooms and videos.

Tail-runners are forgotten, damned and lost.

While setting questions for CU and BCCM exams I would take note of attitudinal preparedness more than classroom capability. It was meant for merit testing.

At the invitation from Prof. Anjan Banerji, the head and dean of the journalism department of the Benaras Hindu University I took practical exams. Most results were good, some excellent.

Applied journalism was challenging to me. No less was teaching. And oftentimes did I feel like having philosophical upbeat while taking classes. It was really a divine satisfaction when my students were all attention to me. Journalistic creativity is a sublime individual achievement. Less ignored is the fact the better.

While teaching you have to keep to the book but do not go by it for all time. And when teaching is practice-oriented the interaction with your pupils will be captivating.

Journalism is an objective art with subjective discipline soaring to great heights of factual philosophy when sublimity mixes with divinity. This is the truth, a conviction which got me widespread appreciation from faculties and colleagues.

Once I had the honour of working as a moderator of questions in the SLET examination run by the West Bengal College Service Commission. Prof. Nityananda Saha, its chairman then, was all praise for my bent.

English was the teaching medium both at CU and BCCM. Questions used to be set in English and answers also were to be written in the same language. But to my utter dismay I found most students got poor marks because their English was poor. I spearheaded a strong campaign for writing answers in Bengali if a candidate so desired. CU accepted my point, so did BCCM.

BHU once invited me to join its journalism faculty as a reader, but I declined the offer. Did I do wrong in not accepting this teaching assignment?

My divinity within has the answer.

8

SYLVAN PROFILE

The life of a newspaper maker is ever a fast life, an inthing that gives him little respite from the daily grind. His moments are prosaic, from the morning hours until finish at dead of night, always looking over the shoulders of fellow-people for a production, tidy and perfect.

After putting the newspaper to bed, the man at the head may go to bed, but the severe pangs of birth will hardly allow him to sleep, his tensions pervading him until the hot or cold cake is in his hand. And, after leafing through the pages of his brain-child, if he finds all is well, only then it all ends well, although the morning after, during the conference-room post-mortem, he is a nervy lot.

My mornings, too, were giddy as nights had been sleepless, with all my anxieties drowning my divinity so deep within that I would have to grope for some shiny beads. And, perhaps, there would not be any bliss in the fathomless bottom.

But some mornings were sunny.

Yet I chose journalism as my career defying my father for which probably the roads of my life ahead were .bumpy. And, furthermore, I went in for teaching indeed after the death of my father which, let me hope so, he did not mind. He was above this earthliness, wasn't he?

Journalism is a profession that is possessive. And obsessive, too. With no escape route from the daily grind. For me as well there was no road sign : Relax.

No mercy from divinity within?

For the exhaustive times with my newspaper work away in Kolkata my sylvan profile got a severe jolt and I turned out to be a robust junk forcing me to shed my frisky romantic bent.

To keep the green in journalism I lost the green in me, and so did Usha. No longer playful as we were, we stopped singing; no longer waiting in the wings for late-night homing, we stopped talking. Our life became lacklustre, with growing grey hair so soon we lost the smiling charm that had been our pride ever since our wedding.

Still utterly helpless I was not; to my wonder, there had been some left-over of the intense romantic fervour I had enjoyed. Only Usha became a victim of urban ruthlessness, yet whenever she went to my village she felt a little more jubilant. Her greying hair appeared to have surrendered to her one-time youthful vigour. But I was happy at my ageless fight against my ageing. My sylvan green remained mostly sharp in my profile, rather having been pepped by my urban sojourn.

My inborn rustic etching could not eat away my love for sylvan beauty, thereby maintaining my ego-balance and eco-order, mercifully holding back my slip into the unromantic morass.

It had been green in my village, green in crop fields, green in cattle pastures, green in forest trees, green in bamboo verges and green in playgrounds. How green was my village one would wonder! But, on the contrary, my city, though not as barren as of today, had the *maidan*, some playfields, some avenues with treelines adoring them, the zoological garden with the botanical beauty on the other side of the flowing Hooghly and some green lawn-grass palaces.

Even then, compared to my village the city was not a greenery. Ecological problem was not the talk of the day as it is becoming today, as pollution is getting over speedily. Still the sweet village air has the smell of the green foliage and field.

The distance between Bengal's village of Charghat is far and wide with the city of Rio in Brazil, but the latter's obsession with pollution is too formidable. Rio had to host an international conference of environmentalists while Charghat is free from eco-crisis as yet. It is sheer luck my village green has not yet been in banishment, though a little fade with the times.

Habitats are fast growing, yet timber-mongers who are about have not been able to swallow the green as they are doing to north Bengal. Ever-alert people of the south have saved the Silent Valley in faraway Kerala from the hellish extinction. Eco-demons are active in the Narmada Valley or in the Himalayan hills but cannot fully subdue the eco-friendly *Chipko* agitators.

Even for all this my village green has lost some of its lustre because of the population explosion too unkind to break the soft soil for building huts and houses.

Years ago, we the youngsters used to play football on a green patch of field by a forest infested with wild boars. But the other day, as I was standing in the midst of wavy crops, a good old friend of mine now retired form service, just appeared and coming near to me said, 'The playground is lost. Now it is cultivated land'.

I said, 'We've one now at the school.'

'But that is not our old-day memory.'

Bhanjan Chowdhury, nick-named Bhaja, was a giant footballer. I felt sorry for him. His grief was genuine. Still, smilingly, I interjected, 'Well, there are so many paddy fields now'. He also smiled and said, 'Yes, so many; there you mow and graze but don't play.'

A bit poetic was as I said, 'Playing here will be like a slushy symphony that only creates a fury of music.' But Bhaja, as his wont, was prosaic and did not appreciate my fantasy. He just looked at me, in mercy.

I thought it was my divine bliss.

Quickly I changed the subject. Aloud I said, 'Hey, look, the sky is blue – no cloud, no haze, no bird.'

Bhaja looked grave, his feet sunk deep in muddy water. The field was waterlogged, probably irrigated. He suddenly growled, 'Aren't you a man of the earth? Why do you fly when your feet are stuck up?'

Another friend of ours, hefty and mighty Nanda – Nanda Kishore Banerjee – came running to us. He slipped and we laughed.

Angrily he said, 'Are you members of a laughing club?'

Again we laughed. 'Yes, we are.'

Nanda looked grave. He had been to the market to buy sweetmeats. He was so hungry. As usual. While gulping them he spotted us half-covered in mud. He then started running to meet us. He got tired and paused for a moment. And then he burst out, 'Why were you two looking up and down? Are you sad?'

'Yes, right you're. There's no playing ground.'

He blared and said, 'Are you mad? We're old, too old. For us it's all work and no play.'

'What?'

'Forget about the days we had.'

'Right.' Bhaja said, 'Those were the days. But now we're too old to play football. We can at the most play cards or chess.'

Laughingly, I sang out the sweetest song that tells of saddest thoughts in my life. And singing came without any effort. Sadder, I was wiser. Was this, wisdom, a divine blessing?

While returning from the non-playing field I began talking again of the sylvan surroundings at the bazar. There was a big mango garden on the western side of the bazar inside which was located the office and resting places of zamindar Bimal Chandra Sinha, once a West Bengal minister. Now the garden is a barren marketplace. To the eastern side of the road that ran dividing the market there was another big mango and coconut garden. Now shops have come up so many, eating up the green there. Behind the bazar there would flow a big river, its banks lined up with green trees; at present more than half of the trees have been felled. And yonder, in the south-east, yet another garden complex having a variety of trees, mostly towering high, was a beauty to enjoy. That, too, has disappeared yielding place to rows of hutments.

Nanda lamented.

But soon our talking point changed. We became sad at losing our garden rendezvous for playing the prankish game of *nashtachandra*, a fun-and-play game on tree tops eating the fruits at will. Our younger generation does not have green pasture-forests, and if there is any it is well guarded to prevent entry of the new-genre greedy. The game is now the thing of the forgotten past.

So is past the thing of the bravado.

And the blessed naughty souls.

The play in the green shades of trees and forests sometimes

took bad turns when our lives were in danger. One such incident I would not forget. One afternoon, when all was quiet and tree leaves were not moving even in thin air, Gantu –Amit Banerjee, a relation of mine—climbed a coconut tree leaning by the side of a pond half shallow and muddy, with a *dao* in hand. He wanted to drink green coconut water to quench his summer- thirst. He was all alone. He went to the top and was about to cut a bunch when a big poisonous snake jumped out and spread its fang hissing. Startled, Gantu lost no time to hit the serpent with his weapon literally beheading it. The head fell down into the pond followed by the coiled body all profusely bleeding. The water at once turned red while Gantu turned blue in horror. He was trembling but could hang on to the tree for some time. Then he fell down by the side of the floating snake.

Gantu might have got the divine bliss, he was safe; but I was wondering how a devil like the cobra could be properly described? Would it be divine? Was it divinity differently manifested?

But surely giving the sleeping father the slip for a noontime rendezvous out of doors under a big mango tree during summer vacation was not a divine blessing. Yet we the two brothers used to do this frequently whenever we felt like enjoying a green mango. We would spread a mat under the shades of the tree just nearby and sitting on it we would bring out a knife to spill off the skin of a mango that had fallen from the tree hit by the wave of a wind and cut into slices, and then after mixing salt and pepper we would slowly eat the spiced pickle. Was the whole thing not a bliss from the green and were we not blessed by.the high blue? And when other boys and girls would come and join us in munching the slices of the godsend-fruit, the bliss became all fun.

Sometimes ripe mangoes fell in the gusty wind, we might enjoy one or two and would take home bagfuls of them, and only then my father, awake in the meantime, took a kind look at them and blessed us by his broad smile. Probably, we would arouse the divinity from his within. Great!

Our village green turned verdant during the rainy season and when the Durga Puja time would come the sylvan lushness became eye-soothing. The *mandap* had trees all around. Chirping birds greeted the daybreak in all glory while the sunset setting had the blessings of the moon. And because of the trees surrounding the worship area the air got cool and hilarious.

Vijaja Dashami was a real treat for all, young and old. Along with the images placed balancingly on two boats tied up side by side we would have boat trips on the swollen river hedged by green trees, bushes and grasses. After immersion, in the twilight evening, we would assemble at the *mandap* to pay our obeisance to the mother goddess hoping for her eternal blessings. We would then go home, get well dressed and offer our *pranams* to parents and deities. The moonlit night was ours, embracing one another irrespective of caste, creed and religion, all raised to the divine upland.

The winter holidays brought us chill and cold and were not as romantic as in the green time. Still we would spend time eating sugarcane, lobster and cauliflower. Green vegetables were in abundance.

This sylvan profile of mine ebbed with the growing up in age, my rustic romanticism quaintly losing ground to urban formality. My dresses changed; my tongues changed; my attitudes changed; and my lifestyles changed. Yet at times, in spirit, I became young but not so, in age; and my glossing over the old golden times continued to be pleasant.

My urban upbringing made me formally urbane but the kind of courtesy I had learnt in the city did not erode my rustic modesty.

What I gained was the democratic way of living possibly because my divine mind got refined, yet for furbishing my love for the water-bathed green on the strand I would often visit the *maidan* and Outram Ghat.

Once I crossed the limit of humility and that was during the Saraswati Puja when I made a mockery of divine worship, ruining my academic proficiency.

Was it a superstition? Perhaps, it was so. And the end-result of such impertinence on my behalf was the ignominy I suffered in the exam.

Perhaps, my insolence persisted even after I got the drubbing from divinity. With the money saved from the *puja* I organised a picnic at Konnagar kissed by the river Ganga. But it was not a holy act of mine and after our return from the trip I submissively received a thrash from the elders of the Udayan Club – the organiser. 'Why don't you do all this with your own contributions' – was the snubbing.

The lesson I learnt the hard way was even with divinity within its bliss is not easily attainable. What is necessary for its unfoldment is respect.

My craze for outing and eating out subsided though it did not die down. I controlled myself in the city, but while in the village I remained the same man often gathering on the grassy banks of the Yamuna for day-long *choruibhati*. And our womenfolks would sit on the kutcha road to the river and enjoy the winter *ghatpalani,* although the wintry winds coming form the north-east side of the river shook everybody to the bone.

Today the village and its inhabitants have had a ghastly change of face with the marketplace, its din and bustle and cash-nexus, destroying the sobriety of traditional relationships between man and man. What has emerged is co-education and disculture, not co-existence and harmony.

For lack of divine environ the village appeared less green than it was early.

9

GOING PLACES (I)

Fond of travel we both were, in our prime time and even today. Whenever chanees came, we just jumped on the idea; but the routine of our going places was rhythmical – not once in a blue moon but once in a year, very modestly speaking.

For me travelling was part of the game, being of immense help to see and read newsy ongoings, far and near. To Usha it has always been a euphoric pleasure, from idea to idea, from fact to fact; but to me it is more of a seeing-through inasmuch as my journalistic prusuit demands.

Going places was my professional practice while for Usha it was the kind of a pilgrimage. Generally, on official outgoings she did not accompany me, but else she lost no time in packing up. All this she would do giggling. Often did I wonder wherefrom she got such a superb energy. Did her divinity within manifest itself that way?

In my case, often tired of deskwork drudgery, I planned escape routes out to nature and beauty, intended to slacken my muscle, nerve and mind; and Usha rose as usual at dawn and by the twilight she would be miles away enjoying the breeze under the stars.

Barring my job-oriented tours, though seldom taken as my sedentary work did not so permit, all the other dash-outs had the divine perceptions of keeping fit, in letter and in spirit of life.

Our tours virtually covered the expanse of India – from Kashmir to Kanyakumari and between Kolkata and Mumbai, the Himalayas drawing us near with snowy peaks waving from horizon to horizon and the seas awesomely inviting us to show how they wash shorelines. Just so wonderful!

To some places I went alone while to some others Usha went alone.

Then a B.A. student in Calcutta University, I accompanied my friend Mohit Kumar Sadhukhan (Banka), then doing his electrical engineering at Jadavpur University, to holy Hardwar. My journalistic acumen was there in me then; yet I was not a professional and so I did not write home about anything that was splendid in the place washed clean by the sacred waters of the swift-running Ganga.

Two years afterwards, I visited with my friend Santosh, a businessman, the hill station Darjeeling, only to be enchanted by the majestic Kanchenjunga. And months later, we the three friends – Santosh, Nitai and myself – went to the long sandy beach of Puri intending to be nurtured by the splashy waves of the sea.

As a working journalist I attended an all-India conference of fellow-travellers in Hyderabad. Usha did not go. While staying there I had the opportunity to see the Golconda Fort nearby and found it had been built amazingly to help send out signals to the throne by just clapping at the main gate. Also did I enjoy the wavy waters of the Hussain Sagar separating the twin cities, Hyderabad and Secunderabad. The tall statue of Lord Buddha which adorns the Sagar today, was not then installed. Char Minar and Saler Jung Museum charmed me.

From Hyderabad I went to Aurangabad to have a glimpse of the historic Ellora and Ajanta. At Ellora the stone carvings of Lord Buddha stood out as outstanding creations. A full temple was made out of a single hill.

On the way back the open-air tomb of Emperor Aurangzeb came by. And also the Daulatabad Fort which I climbed to the top. The dark-brown replica of Agra's white-marvelled Taj could be seen from the bus as it went by.

By bus next morning I went to have a beautiful view of the Ajanta caves, their walls decorated with murals and frescos, besides a reclining yet lively image of Lord Buddha. All beauties were captivating sending out godly vibrations all over, the small waterfall falling from a cave-hole producing a continuous song in silence.

And to some places Usha went alone accompanying other tourist-batches, such as to Pashupatinath in Kathmandu, Nepal, to Kedarnath and Badrinath; and also to Guwahati, Shillong and Cherapunji, besides the Kamakshya temple overlooking the mighty Brahmaputra.

Incidentally, Usha accompained me to Pondicherry once and we spent a few hours there before returning to Chennai. But, later, along with some of her friends she had been to Pondicherry spending a few days and enjoying the life divine.

Seeing is enjoying. But just that? No. It is as well believing in the all-pervasive divine spirit. And belief leads to bliss.

Away in Kashmir where the great Himalaya showers its blessings in bounty we together went along with our younger son Arya, leaving behind daughter Tanima, already married, and elder son Saumya, busy elsewhere.

Spending time in salubrious coolness overseen by the shady chinar and chestnut trees spread around the snowy hillsides with dwarf applevines offering fruits aplenty was a wonderful thrill for all of us.

The Dal Lake in Srinagar with *shikaras* and speed-boats moving hither and thither with gaily dressed people on them was an inviting divine spectacle. We had been to several places of scenic grandeur never failing in attractions that changed every moment of life with astounding joy. At Pahalgam, the gateway to the holy cave Amarnath, gave Arya a joyride on horseback to the golf green kissed by the Lidder full of swift-current rapids; at Sonemarg, far down north in the depth of towering snow-caps, where we were a bit late in arriving, we sat down taking our food bathing in the bright sunshine while Arya quickly munching his meat jumped on to a horse and sped off to see the glacier on the hilly top; at Gulmarg we all enjoyed horseride to the glacier high up in the bluish snows; and at Kokernag we spent the chilly night shaken to the bone though fully covered by two or three blankets yet charmed by the aroma of flowers of several colours, while at Anantnag we roamed about buying cratefuls of red, yellow and green apples.

Unless one had the divine propulsion one will not have the bliss of going places, from corner to corner, and the time, too, was miserly. We did not see the Sankaracharya temple on the hilltop in the very heart of Srinagar, nor did we have the luck then to visit the uphill shrine of Vaishnodevi near Katra although we passed through Jammu.

Similarly, many places of exotic beauty have remained unseen. The Kargil and Ladakh belt is one such.

Lately, we both made it to Vaishnodevi. It was an uphill journey which we did on horseback. But it was our folly to take the downhill trip on foot, since after covering a few kilometres we felt dog-tired, Usha limping with the swollen knee and me with the jammed knee. Still the journey was highly blissful getting enough opportunities to meet endless flows of devout people and to see the snow-filled or cloud-filled bounties of godly nature.

On the way back, downwards to Amritsar, we visited Dharamsala and Dalhousie and were enthralled to see the wavy peaks, the tall trees, the Dalai Lama's seat of prayers, the Chamba and Kangra valleys, the Jwalamukhi-Shaktipith, the Bajreswarpith, and the Bollywood shooting spot at Khajier.

And the Golden Temple at Amritsar appeared to us a heavenly wonder on earth. Twice we visited it, not yet sated.

Chandigarh has the warmth of a new-life city built by French architect Le Corbousier. Twice we together went there and our visits were blessed by the serene beauty of the Sukhna Lake pitted against the great Himalayan wall.

Simla, a hill station of northern India,beckoned us to its cool heights when we visited it on the Diwali night showing off its garlands of light. It was also Kali Puja night, the Kalibari adorned with multi-coloured bulbs. The hill-night was chilly but the daytime on the Mall had a life buoyantly splendid.

But, sorry, Kulu, Manali, Rohtang Pass and Kinnaur remained beyond our reach.

Meanwhile, I had been lucky to visit Bhakra Nangal and Govind Sagar. The dam was a grand spectacle; it looked as though it was a high waterfall, the waters falling far down below from a height that almost met the sky, with Govind Sagar full to the brim seemingly belching out of the deep belly of skirting hills.

Along with Usha I once went to Delhi. In the party were my

family, all together, and some other relations. We put up at Kalibari and toured several places like the Qutab Minar, the Red Fort, the Jama Masjid, the Jantar Mantar, the Purana Qilla and the Humayun's Tomb, besides other buildings of modern historic interest.

From there we the entire batch went southward to visit the twin Pauranic towns of Mathura and Vrindaban, with the Yamuna river flowing by echoing the divine music of Lord Krishna.

Furtherward, it was the famous Taj Mahal which we saw in wonder; washed clean and dazzling the Taj appeared to us, after the clouds dispersed and the Kojagari Purnima moon shone, as a bright marvel of excellence, the coloured stone chips carved in the magnificent structure glaring the thousands of peeping eyes. The moments were an unforgettable legend.

From Agra the next destination, though very short, was Fatehpuri Sikri, where the Buland Darwaza stood like a pompous gateway to Emperor Akbar's Hindu Queen Jodha Bai's *mahal.* Inside a hall the fine marble-cut lattice work by master craftsmen could draw superlatives in its description.

And at Agra, too, there is a big fort built by the Emperor Shahjahan where he was himself a prisoner later and in the room just above the Yamuna flowing to the Taj was there a stone placed in the window through which the old disillusioned emperor would see his Mumtaj memorial. Now the stone is missing.

From Agra to Lucknow was not a hazardous journey, but our stay there in the house of a near relation was really pleasant. Our tour of the city in tongas from labyrinthine Bhulbhulaiya to the Gomti riverside became a heritage trip, old buildings mixing with new rises making a cultural blend that transcended reason for the mean political division of religion. Today the picture is different.

At Ayodhya we did not halt for spending nights and sightseeing; we skipped the place for hurrying to the holy places of Viswanath – Varanasi. That did not mean we ignored the Ramtirtha and the Babri Masjid atop it. We just bypassed politics.

For three nights we spent there we saw the temple of Lord Viswanath, besides, visiting other places of worship. We went to the Dashashyamedh Ghat and took holy dips in the ever-flowing sacredness of the 'northward' Ganga. By hiring boats we rowed up and down seeing the *ghats* in a row, including the Monicornica Ghat, the crematorium.

The umbrellas, the *sannyasins* in meditation, the countless bathers, the peacocks, the beggars, and the boats – all excelling everything else in the eternal beauty treatment of the place of pilgrimage.

Usha was beaming with smile and joy.

It was a rainy time when an opportunity came by as I was invited by the Benaras Hindu University, for a flying visit, to take the written and oral exams in journalism in the campus. After the assignment was over, I took an autorickshaw to reach the road that was leading to the Dashashyamedh Ghat. The rain-drenched Ganga was in fury, full to the brim, the currents lashing the steps and driving out the few bathers in a huff.

Then, before the sun dropped down the Ganga, I saw the Lord and offered my humble prayers. When I touched the head of the idol I felt within me a serious shock that electrified me for moments. The shock was divine, my within pulsating with the sensation of an inspired life.

We took, on the earlier visit, a car for going to Sarnath to see the excavation work related to Lord Budha. It was a capivating sight. From there we went to Ramnagar, on the other side of the river, to see a palace.

Away, in the south-western canopy upstream, there is the Prayagtirtha, where at the Sangam confluence three great rivers have met, of which the Ganga and the Yamuna are visible but the Saraswati is not. The Yamuna waters are deep and green while the Ganga is a bit shallow and muddy, its swirling waters running fast to wash the sacred feet of Lord Viswanath.

A recent satellite picture of the Saraswati course is reported to be showing that the river could be located away in the Thar desert adjoining the Aravalli range of hills, hidden under the brownish sand.

But at the Prayag confluence this river does not have any existence, down under or above the soil.

Still the Triveni Sangam is a great holy place for divine salvation, only to be so realised after soothing baths.

Usha was not blessed by dips in the Kumbh Mela, Prayag, but she was fortunate in having the blessings at the one at Hardwar.

A tragic stampede took many lives from the mother earth's loving lap during this *mela,* but as luck would have it, Usha remained alive as she had been just a few metres away from the cross-feet.

And I knew Hardwar has a great divine power at least for me and Usha, not any subjective dissonance of mine.

Once we had been to Kumaon and Garhwal hills. In the first half, our journey began at the Delhi ISBT for long hours of the wonderful bus trip to Haldwani and Kathgodam. Haldwani is a busy trading centre while Kathgodam is just at the foothills overlooking the Kumaon range with green trees abounding on hilltops. From Kathgodam we changed from the big bus to a smaller one, suitable for the winding route on the hill.

The ripples on the otherwise placid waters of Nainital were rhythmically sparkling but chilly indicating that wintry winds were blowing from a curbed gap of the hills on the north. We had a little difficulty in finding our government hotel, but after we were in and had tea with snacks, we felt warm. We came down to the grassy lawn, spread chairs and started talking shop forgetting the shiver down the spine.

Down south of the lake there was no hill, the nice cut-out showing us the downslide distance, someone saying there are Bhimtal and Sattal. Our tour programme had been fixed earlier, yet we included the two *tals* (lakes) in the itinerary.

By the flanking banks of the Nainital lake there are two highrise hills, one side fully green intercepted by the Sherwood College campus and on the other side, just facing it, the array of houses and hotels with people jostling around in groups and couples, all winter-dressed to the full, all drinking cokes and eating chocolates and all cracking jokes in playful glee.

The following morning was bright and sunny; we first climbed the ropeway to reach the China Peak and see the distant snow-capped tips of the Himalayas. It was superb grandeur all round.

Form the ropeway we had a grand view of the lake below stilled in silence.

After *darshan* at the Naini mandir and going shopping for an hour to two, we hired a boat for a smooth ride on the lake waters sparkling with the falling light of the sun and mirroring the neons, bulbs and tubes glowing in rows of excellence on the reclining hill over the mall.

Next day, at nine in the morning, our bus left for Almora another hill station full of intense vibrations blessed by the presence of Swami Vivekananda during his *paribrajak* days. The meandering road to the hill resort appeared smooth for which we had a pleasant trip up and down the hills, and by the late afternoon the bus stopped in front of our government hotel. We were too hungry to spend time at the reception; we could make ourselves comfortable in our room after we had our lunch with boiled veg and mutton stew as our dishes.

As the sunlight became brown we came out on the green lawn downstairs and looked yonder at the creamy waves high in the mountainous range. I told Usha, 'See the wonder'. Usha just took a look and said early in the morning tomorrow the scene would be more wonderful. Then we went in and had tea.

The following dawn was simply fantastic. We had got up earlier and from the windows enjoyed the unforgettable spectacle. We saw K-2, Mana and Trishul, all colourfully eye-soothing. After taking a round at the marketplace we fulfilled another mission of ours by visiting the Ramakrishna Mission Ashrama and had veg lunch while talking about Boshi Sen, who had been long associated with the development of Almora. By the way, we had *dahi* at lunch, a delicacy for me for years.

The reservation done in the bus for Kausani leaving the town next morning, we roamed about seeing things and people in shops.

The bus took a semi-circuitous route to proceed towards Kausani for which we did have an eyeful of hilly beauty, with a gorge deep down touching a threadlike yet swirling river virtually dividing the town-walls.

By eleven in the forenoon the bus stopped at the terminus-level of Kausani and we got down bag and baggage. We thought there would be a jeep waiting for taking the visitors uphill to our resthouse that faces the Himalayan range from a distance seemingly at an arm's length. But we were disappointed as there was no jeep.

Hiring a coolie we were climbing the hilly path, Usha grousing and gasping. All of a sudden, as though a godsend, an army jeep appeared and the coolie waved his hand and helped us to get into the vehicle which had stopped out of sheer kindness.

The hotel room provided us with enough leg space and the adjoining verandah where we stood for some time opened up a panoramic vista of eternal beauty, with the Kedarnath peak seen at the far western end and Pancholi in the east. The Badrinath peak Nilkantha, the Hathi peak shadowing the K-2 and Mana, the Nandaghunti, the Trishul, the Nandadevi and Nandakot, and some other unnamed peaks came in between. On the way we had passed by the Gandhi Ashram from where also the panorama of beauty was well visible, but not as widely as it was from the Kausani hotel-top.

Malay Gupta, a bank economist, and family became friendly to us, and we all together made our journey to Ranikhet highly enjoyable. We had earlier bookings at the government hotel complex a little distance away from the bus station. Contacted immediately on the telephone, the hotel management sent a car for our 'home-coming', as it was so described. The hotel is a nice place to stay in, surrounded by forests and hills. We had tea and took an evening stroll amid split rays of the sun, the flocking, frolicking birds chirping music without a stop.

Back in the hotel we together talked with the driver of the car which had brought us from the bus station and hurriedly fixed up our next day's programme of tour by the same car. The day after, too, we booked the car for our trip to Sattal (seven lakes), Bhimtal and Nainital. Atop the Ranikhet hill we visited the Kali temple and some half a century kilometres away we saw a picturesque temple of Mata Durga, built over a thousand years ago.

Ranikhet at night looked bright, highly illuminated, but we could not enjoy the sight for long as we took our dinner early just to lie on bed and sleep tired.

The morning seemed to come early next day and by that time we were all up and ready for the journey. After the breakfast we drove past the sun-bathed forests crossing the town parameter in half an hour. Thence we were on the road downhill and bypassing both Nainital and Almora we came down to Sattal at first and finally to Bhimtal, a vast expanse of water skirted by low hills. Straightway we went to the government resort where we had earlier booking for lunch. The meat-dish lunch over, we came out on the lawn to get a wide view of the lake, a splendid scene full of motor boats playing all over leisurely.

At the late afternoon we left Bhimtal in the car leaving behind our new friends who had the booking for night stay. We were bound for Nainital for two more days' stay at the same hotel where we had left some kits and luggage.

With scores of holidayers wandering aimlessly about the hill-lake town looked the same charming to us. The wind was little colder than in the previous week. We also got mixed with the strollers and gossipers around and had sumptuous dinner at a wayside restaurant. Next day, after a lavish breakfast, we spent the entire time outing along the shops and on the strand.

Before twilight I went inside the transport office to book our seats for Hardwar via Jim Corbett garden. The bus would leave the stand at nine in the morning, so we would arrive at the bay in time for boarding it. We had little concern about our accommodation for we had reservations, but when we tried to get into the bus we found it jammed beyond capacity. The bus conductor readily came to our rescue and we got seats, as earlier confirmed.

It was a long, long way to Hardwar, our arrival time there being four in the afternoon. Where would we take our lunch? At Ramgarh, the conductor said: And tea, miles afterwards. We just relaxed.

At Ramgarh we had some snacks, not liked by Usha, and some *lichis,* all sour. And thereafter at a wayside stall we had glassfuls of *lassi* giving us the required cold in our body systems.

We had been journeying for hours from the cold climate to the hot weather, the change taking place so quickly that eco-adjustments were quite difficult to achieve.

By four, under the burning sun, we were at Hardwar; the Ganga in all its fury was running fast without altering the barometer in the least. Getting down at the bus station we hired a rickshaw to find a lodge for our three-day stay in the holy town. We got one after a long search, at a high rate. Relaxing for some time we had tea and then moved to Har-ki-Pauri to inhale to our hearts' content the soothing air-current, and at sun-down we awfully enjoyed the Ganga Mata *puja* with blazing *mashals* lighting up the entire *ghat* area to the beat of drums and blowing of conchshells. An unbelievable divinity wonderfully manifested in the faces of a thousand humans, all in prayerful mood and ecstasy. We were no exceptions.

The new thing that I saw this time, Usha by my side, was the ropeway to the Mansha hill, but in the distance away on the other side of the rocky Ganga the bigger Chandi hill looked damp and dark, the river having only the criss-cross of improvised bridges, spanning the bed, built for the lakhs of pilgrims to use during the last Kumbh mela.

Some short visits we made to Rishikesh and beyond Lakshmanjhula and Ramjhula across the river, hanging under the weight of men, women and children. A ferry launch had been pressed into service for those who were averse to suspension.

When I had come to Lakshmanjhula earlier with Banka I did not find the new *jhula* named Ramjhula.

After three days' stay at Hardwar and holy dips in the Ganga at Brahmakundu, we went to Dehradun and stayed in the house of Saumya's friend Tablu, then a senior chemist in ONGC. It was rather a gala time for us all. However, Tablu took his car out for the visit to Sahasradhara, a hill-slope of a thousand springs all spilling into a flow cutting its way through stones and boulders raising a sound of music and leaving a sweet refrain in ears.

One morning we went to Mussoorie, the exotic hill station at a looking distance from Dehradun. We spent the whole day circling in a four-man driven rickshaw the hill and the mall; climbing the gun-hill table by a ropeway, wherefrom we had a wide-range view of the waves of mountains touching the white-cap peaks far beyond; and just walking around in leisure. The night was cold but not chilly with the starlit sprawl of heavenly Dehradun down below being a warm-up beauty-treat.

10

GOING PLACES (II)

Coastal India has a conical look, its sea-beaches luring millions into their sand and sun. Most of the beaches we two enjoyed from Digha to Juhu, looking at the vast expanses of water turning from grey to blue near the distant horizons, everywhere in enigmatic wonder.

But the shores of Dwarka, Kovalam, Chandipur and Gopalpur have remained virgins. To us.

The treelined Digha beach in West Bengal is sandy yet stony while Puri in Orissa, the land of Lord Jagannath, has a charming sandy beach, the stretch being constantly lashed by curling breakers, foaming yet not fuming.

In my early visit I used to swim into wavy depths holding the hand of a *nulliah,* but later with Usha beside me, I just whiled away my time sitting on the wet sand and enjoying the low splashy surfs.

The Waltair beach at Visakhapatnam in Andhra is rocky except for the narrow Ramakrishna stretch which was so inviting that I dared to walk on it alone, Usha not accompanying me to inhale the breeze.

Further south the Marina beach at Chennai is vast, but we did not have our bath although several danger spots had been fenced off with proper warnings. And the breakers were not as high and curly as in Puri. The beach in Pondicherry, the meditation land of

Sri Aurobindo, makes a splash and kisses the sand in groans. The waves were rhythmical, yet we did not respond to the divine call.

From Madurai we journeyed to Rameshwaram, the train crossing the bridge, as though through the waves of the sea. It was still dark when we reached the station. Hiring a tonga we came to the government lodge just standing on the shore where we found even at the shady hour of the dawn several people bathing in the shallow and dirty beach. At a distance the Dhanuskoti stretch into the sea could be seen. Lord Rama was known to use this tip to build a bridge over the sea to cross over to Lanka for freeing Sita from the clutches of Ravana. That bridge is no longer there since the stretch has been ravaged by a storm. Now a road bridge has come up on the Rameshwaram stretch.

Atop a small hill, a few short hops away, our tonga took us whereto, we saw the cement print of the Lord's feet directed towards Lanka. From there we travelled to see the great temple at Rameshwaram which has long corridors neatly hanging on pillars. The spell was magnetic.

High waves of the three seas meet at the bottom tip of mother India where located is Kanyakumari and a little away in the south the Vivekananda Rock Memorial blessed by the memory of the wandering saint and from where he looked into the West to be present at the historic Parliament of Religions held towards the end of the nineteenth century at Chicago where he cast his spell by calling the children of America as his sisters and brothers.

A look into the lower landscape of our motherland gave us a wonderful feeling. A white-painted church that peeped out of several multi-coloured houses peopled by different religious sects opened up our eyes on the sunlit hue of the multi-faceted life where divinity in oneness reigns supreme.

Kovalam, the wonder beach in Thiruvanantapuram, we missed for we were short of time. We were denied the bliss of the shady sea with the reclining coconut trees kissing the paddle boats in an air of serene joy. We did not have the tossing merriment on the low sea with birds flying in formation in the hope of getting food leftovers.

The beaches in Goa are varied, some sandy, some rocky, and of them the Calungute shoreline is a stretch of breezy beauty washed by surfs and kissed by breakers. We walked along together on the wet sand, the cottages standing by in a row under the green coconut trees whose leaves were flying like flags atop the swinging heads, the birds with their wings spread getting no chance to have a perching foothold. Even to some other beaches we did go and found hippies mostly lying nude, men and women in clusters. Was this love divine? Or was it a 'sexpo'?

Further up in the north the Juhu beach in Mumbai is a whopping sprawl, horizon to horizon, the sea washing the blessed feet of the mother country bending low in a submissive devotion. We enjoyed a horse-drawn tongaride, soft sandy clay spattering our dresses; but, ill luck, we did not have the blessing of seeing the made-up faces of the tinsel town hero-heroine machos.

Away from the seas and mountains, in criss-cross, yet somewhere undulating, midlands and plains, we toured a number of places but missed as many. Towards the south we skipped Ooty and Kodaikanal, but we made to Mysore, Bangalore and Tirupati. Going round Mysore the land of Tipu Sultan was a pleasure and the Vrindaban Gardens a star-lit Eden. Bangalore is a lovable terrain while our trip to Tirupati was a delightful bliss that showered on us from under the golden dome of the shrine.

Ellora apart, the Ajanta caves that we saw in great wonder, struck a sorry note in our awful minds for, since my solitary visit years ago, we did not have euphoric happiness by looking at the damaged wall-paintings as a result of rain-water seepage and bad upkeep, or better said, out of sheer neglect for years and ages. Archeologists from Delhi had been trying hard to restore the damaged portions of the murals and frescos either by covering them with glass or by repainting with chemicals. It appeared to me that natural colouring was a problem since cave paintings had colours made from natural leaves and skins of trees, and chemical colours did not fit in with them. So the mixing or retouching was a disaster.

Is the Buddhist divine *nirvana* lost in inorganic elements? In a culture in which chemistry is getting the better of naturalism?

Back in Mumbai again, we must say we had only a week's card in the city of Gateway to India, although Usha afterwards had to stay there for so many months, however, with breaks in between.

It was during the illness of my younger daughter-in-law. But I had one chance. Only.

The Elephanta Caves though I saw by travelling on the sea gave us an idea about how the old-time builders could get for the later genre a plethora of wonderful creations. We have had so many cave-cultures built so assiduously away from the eagle eyes of destruction, from Ajanta to Elephanta to Mahaballipuram to Khandagiri, to mention only a few novelties.

From the Elephanta Caves we could have a long-shot view of the Tarapur Atomic Reactor Plant dome. Is it not like the Sivalingam, the mythological energy symbol? A wishful thinking! A divine paradox!

We had made trips to other places, too, during our short stay in Mumbai, yet I for one did not have the great feel of life. The Marine Drive, the Malabar Hills, the Worli milk booth and so many other places of high interest attracted us. The architectural beauty of the Victoria Terminus railhead was in a word splendid. And the skyline all along the shorefront was an eyeful of towering modernity, by and large.

But the sea voyage in a large ship from Mumbai Port to Panaji, the capital town of Goa, annexed from Portugal during the post-independence period, gave our morale a big boost. The sunset from the cabin-deck of the ship, the flash-lighted Ratnagiri stop-over, and the cruise along the coast far away on the sunny dawn enlivened us with memorable dreams, and finally, the silent entry into the Mandovi river at the mouth of the port capital opened up a new vista of life which had been unknown to us so long, and our faces were beamy.

The government hotel at Panaji, just overlooking the flowing river, provided us with enough room for rest, relaxation and rejuvenation. Losing no time for a good catnap we moved out walking the distance to the sea where the sun was still burning out the western sky, but as we took strolls under the trees our shadows lengthened. We then decided to return to the hotel for tea. That night we had our dinner out; the crab-dish was really a delicacy for us.

After a good sleep at night we got up early to see the red glow of the rising sun over the Mandovi bridge now and then intercepted by passing cars, buses and trucks. The breakfast over, we boarded a luxury coach for conducted tours of north and south Goa.

Goa has an undulating terrain interspersed by low hills, cultivated plains, brown mines, green forests and interlacing rivers, all blessed by the surfing sea. And the villages, especially in deep areas, resemble those in Bengal even for the climatic difference.

We saw Marmagoa, Vasco da Gama and the church where the embalmed body of St. Francis Xavier lies in state. A fort turned jail we found standing on the rocks facing the Arabian Sea.

Our night journey by a deluxe bus from Panaji to Pune via Kolhapur was not as comfortable as we thought of – it was a sleepless night for me though Usha sitting by me dozed and snored most of the time. Pune brightened up by the rising sun was picturesque soothing our tensed nerves as we got down outside our hotel.

After having smart showers in tepid water and then an omelette-bread-snacks breakfast, we slipped out of the hotel to have a close look at the city walking all the time and munching green *chanas*. We inquired about Osho's *ashrama* but nobody seemed to be in a mood to enlighten us. They were tight-lipped, but why?

Mahabaleshwar, high on the hills by Bombay Road, we did by the early morning bus form Pune. The haze had not cleared, Chhatrapati Shivaji's abode was above the cliffs, and it was a long journey taking four to five hours to reach the historic place. There the Ma Bhavani Mandir is located. Shivaji used to bend low before the mother goddess to have her divine blessings for fighting the Moghul intruders.

A normal human being though I am, I knelt down in front of the living idol with folded hands and keeping my eyes shut I looked through within and sought her bliss. An awful silence prevailed.

After lunch, we moved out and went to the other side of skirting hills where Arthur's Table was 'spread' hanging from a dizzy height, far above a deep gorge.

The afternoon air was cool. Shivaji, too, kept cool while fighting wicked Afzal Khan with *baghnokh*. The sun shone bright. So did shine Shivaji with a blazing glory.

Late in the evening we returned to Pune. After an hour's rest we had dinner to retire early for preparing to leave for Aurangabad by bus past midnight; but I did not get a wink of sleep though Usha's usual snoring could well be heard.

The bus came at the right time. We entered and reclined in our seats comfortably. The bus gained speed, so the moon, too. As I was awake I could see the moon remained awake, probably on compassionate grounds.

From Aurangabad we went to Ellora at first to see the caves and the wonders within. Midway, on our journey back, we saw the latticed open-sky tomb of Aurangzeb. Then we halted at Daulatabad to climb the fort, but we made half of the uphill walk, though, as I recollected, I made it fully during my first trip to history.

Next day, after our visit to the Ajanta memories, we got into another bus bound for Jalgaon. The wide road runs paralled to the one on the hill range of the Western Ghats blocking the sunshine and cooling the air.

In a hotel at Jalgaon we spent the night and in the forenoon the following day we were at Bhusawal. For two nights we took rest at an AC retiring room at the station, me sleepless hearing engine whistles and counting train movements. At dawn the following day, when it was still dark, we left by Bombay Mail, our destination Jabalpur.

Jabalpur is a well laid-out town; we were delighted spending hours out of doors, sight-seeing, and nights in a spacious room we had hired earlier through a friend of ours. We had really a splended time.

Hiring a car from morning hours till lunch-time we saw some places of interest, at the first opportunity enjoying the boatride on the Narmada river hedged by off-white marble rocks, all a marvel of nature.

The river, its swirling current gushing out from the waterfall, a few kilometres away, flows through a gorge created by the nature-cut artistry, a beauty that is beyond human imagination. I thought the divinity which remains within man can have manifestations through infinite love, perhaps born of such an ethereal yet earthly interaction.

The waterfall backdrop is wide and shallow, shrubs sprouting scattered, but the mouth from where the water is falling is narrow; the volumes of water are falling deep in thunder, the sparkles producing a haze of a rainbow; into the deep foam some boys were playfully jumping to find the coins thrown by the surrounding people above gleefully clapping with every find.

While row-boating downstream we came by a rocky tip as if raising its head and looking at us in awe. Strangely, we discovered Siva-stone. The boatman stopped and barefooted we climbed the tip to offer our prayers. Oh! It was really a divine pleasure being one with the embodiment of supernatural energy.

From Jabalpur to Khajurao was a long way. The bus covered the distance in eleven hours that included our stops at Maihar and Sethna. Maestro Ustad Alauddin Khan developed Maihar as the seat of music where Ali Akbar Khan and Ravi Shankar learnt their art as the *guru's* true disciples.

It was about sunset when we arrived at the Khajurao temple complex, a grandiose communion of art with beauty sancitified by the divine touch of a godly hand.

The morning light had not yet penetrated the cosy room of the hotel when we got up and quickly ate our breakfast. Usha and myself went out walking a little to have the gradations of wonder in our minds. Small shrines were scattered all over the area, yet they were all great pieces of architectural beauty. Huge magnificent temples were imposing attractions and we spent our time mostly there roaming about, sitting leisurely and keenly enjoying the creative life divine. Giggling Usha suddenly went silent and drew my eyes to an erotic pleasure piece.

I said, 'Why do you think this is erotic? What then do you say about the way of our life?' I paused for a moment and then burst out, 'All the life of ours is sense-friendly, and so erotic, isn't it?' Usha got fazed, did not think I would react so unkindly, and so she decided to keep silent.

But I relented and said softly, 'This is not just eroticism but it is an aesthetic fantasy transcending reason if not perversion.'

Usha corrected herself and spoke out giggling, 'Yes, you're right. It's bewitching, the beauty and the beast together. It's a serene artistry which has been amazingly chiselled giving the basic sensuality a sublime divinity.'

And to her divinity theory I could add something of our worldliness. I said, 'Sex is a part of life which is puritanically divine.'

I made her recollect what she had seen on the outer walls in the temples of Puri, Konark and Bhubaneswar. 'The walls are full of erotic scenes, are'nt they?' I just coaxed her, yet she argued, 'Yes, there're too many of them, but don't forget these lines disappear from the mind the moment we enter sanctum sanctorums. We see the idols then and not the images—the idols of love drown the images of sense.'

A humble question I then put to her—it is a million-dollar question: Is sex then a door to divinity?

From Khajurao we came to Sethna by bus and from Sethna to Allahabad by train. Together we visited the Prayagtirtha and had the divine blessings from our holy dips at the *sangam*.

Our circuitous tour of Rajasthan had a regal flavour but we could not visit Bikaner as we were short of time. We had to skip the fort town to hurry to Agra for home-coming.

From Agra where the journalists from all over the country had met in a conference we started our Rajasthan trip and our first bus-stop was at the Bharatpur circuit house. We made for Deeg, a nice retreat some forty miles away from Bharatpur for the Jat kings. And while returning to our rest-house we saw the famous bird sancturay at Bharatpur and spent some time until the dusk strolling under the greenish woods. It was a jovial time for us in tune with the twittering and singing birds busy flying to their nests.

We also saw some Siberian cranes, in flocks at times, flying low over the brackish water full of hyacinths and weeds, all jostling and flapping along with other birds in a playful mood.

Next morning, with the help of some journalist friends crowding at the bus terminus, we made our entry into the loads of a bus, and fortunately, after a while, got two seats. The bus sped for Jaipur, the capital city of Rajasthan. Nature held out green and blue for our view, all smiles and shiny, but at the bus terminus at Jaipur we were slightly held up for moments for we could not at first solve our accommodation problem. But it was the bliss again, as the luck favoured us after we had a nostalgic homily with the Bengali bus manager. He connected us with the government information director whom we had met at Agra and the officer was good enough to come all the way to the terminus and made for us two reservations in a government hotel.

After lunch we moved out and went to Hawa Mahal and Jaipur Palace for having an inlook into them. All royal attractions and wonders!

When it was dark we went to the well-lit marketplace for shopping.

The morning after, the sun was not rude as our luxury coach made for Amber Palace built by Man Singh, Emperor Akbar's commander-in-chief. Situated on the edge of a low green hill near Jaipur, the exquisite Sheesh Mahal has rows of glass panels mirroring mangled faces of the stream of onlookers. Wide-eyed and awed, we stepped in and out. We had an elephant ride on the compound of the palace. The ride was body-shaking. Finally, we had the *darshan* of Goddess Kali, the idol having been brought from Jashore, the seat of power of Barobhuinya hero Pratapaditya. But was the *darshan* a divine bliss?

At Ajmer, a snug town nicely built on undulating land, we saw the famous *Dargah* of Akbar's Guru, Moin-ud-din Chishti. We went in. My body quivered as I offered prayers. I felt ecstatic but I could not say if it was a divine feeling, or just a perception.

True to life, there is no barrier to realising the very all-pervasive message of religion.

Our next destination was Pushkar, a vast lake of scared waters though covered with weeds, its banks uneven with hilly mounds scattered all over, and on the one side a sandy run-up to a high hill Savitri *Pahar*. A legend has it, the lake was formed by the fall of a meteorite once from the blue. By the side of the holy lake there is the temple of Lord Brahma, the only one such in India.

After taking holy dips I paid obeisance to my fore fathers, Usha joining me in prayers.

Both of us climbed the Savitri hill and got tired but it was rewarding, too. From the top we looked around and had a hazy view of the landscape with sunrays gentled by a cool breeze.

By bus we came down to Ajmer and only then we noticed there is a Durga *Mandir* just by the side of the Dargah Sharif, and I must beg to be excused for overlooking it during the first visit. But what struck me with wonder is how two religions can easily co-exist.

The divine love from everybody's within has in fact got the outer focus!

Chittorgarth, the land of Padmini, the beauty queen, and Mira Bai, the Krishna devotee, is on the top of hilly ranges looking like a vast tableland, with the town-spread touching its rocky and sandy feet. We hired an auto for our upward journey into history.

The mirror which had reflected the bathing beauty of Padmini for whom Alauddin Khilji fell madly in love was still adorning the wall of the room standing high up on the lake. Tourists still looked at it to feel how wonderful was Alauddin's heartthrob.

The mad invader was in illusion, the Jawaharbarata canal still flowing by only mellowed by the refrain of dying beauties.

Vijay Stambha stands erect. We climbed it. The signs of modern vibrant life amidst the verdure in the Rajasthani desert were clearly visible from the top.

Mira's temple was intact but we did not hear her divinely tuneful *bhajans*. Only memories sang out, but we were deaf.

Downhill we came. Only pathos filled in our desolate minds. And the sun was about to set.

Again it was the bus that took us to Udaipur. The road was so smooth that the journey remained comfortable. On the way we heard about Haldighat where Rana Pratap had fought the Moghul valiantly, but we could not negotiate it as the bus took a bypass.

Udaipur, full of ups and downs in a sylvan setting, was cold yet cozy effusing an aroma of royalty spread all over, not only in the city but in the lake; but why it was so miserly in providing us with a room for our stay only for two or three nights we did not understand. However, we overcame the problem, though initial hazards took away much of our time.

Hiring again an auto we went out sight-seeing, at first up the hill and then elsewhere. On a grassy hilltop upland there stood a majestic statue of the Rana on horseback. Adjacent to the hill is the

Nehru Lake, its placid waters touching softly the edges of the Nehru Park. It looks like a floating park negotiable by boat. We looked at it and heaved a sigh as we had little time to rowboat there. And yonder we could see the expanse of Udaipur Lake with the royal palace floating as an island, half now converted into a hotel, all smiling radiantly. A mystic grandeur, indeed! Our boat tossed by the ripples created by a soothing wind gave us an idyllic hallucination.

Our resting place next was Mount Abu where we went after touching Abu Road. It was then the ebbing time of the afternoon. Our hotel was up the hill, a small distance away from the car park. Usha got angry. She did not like staying in a hotel away from the bazar, the hub of life. Entering into the room she just lay down on the foamy bed and slept.

The following morning we boarded a government tourist coach to have an overview of the hill station. At first we saw the wonder-temple Dilwara of the Jains, adorned by stone-sculpted artefacts and then we visited the topmost place in the Aravalli range. Although the top was sun-bathed, we had the cooling air blowing from the distant Arabian Sea. We came downhill and left the coach at the bazar for taking our meals at a wayside restaurant. Then, in the afternoon, a bad time though, we had a boatride in the pulsating lake.

But, after this bonhomie, I just put forward my idea of going back to our hotel for a little rest, before we could start for enjoying the sunset from the western edge of the hill, and this enraged Usha so much that she did go to the hotel-room but never to see the sunset. I failed to persuade her to come out, so I left for sunset-seeing all alone. And naturally it was just a routine sun-down though seen at a low tip of a glaring range far away.

Forlorn I stood glum for a while. It was getting a little dark. Distressed I left the place, and while walking down the hill I asked me about Usha's discomfiture. I tried hard to get a divine meaning of it but in vain. I took the plunge into the depth within me but, bad luck, I got drowned in total darkness. No. divinity!

The morning sun was playing hide and seek with us as we were coming back to Abu Road to catch the bus for Jodhpur. The bus had left Ahmedabad early in the morning and was overcrowded.

It came late. And the jostling at the gate for entry defied discipline. Earlier, I had engaged a porter to push us inward for which I promised him a higher price. Thank God, after our entry with luggage intact, we found one seat in the front was vacant. Usha sat there comfortably, but I had to remain standing. All of a sudden, I located a can beside Usha's seat and after looking around I sat down, none objecting.

The bus sped to Sirohi fast and there a seat fell vacant where I got in. An hour later, we reached Jodhpur, the virtual watershed of the Thar desert. It was noontime, hot and dry.

From the bus station we took an auto to arrive at the portal of a government tourist lodge. Bag and baggage we got down from the vehicle only to be told by the hotel people there was no vacant room because a *barat* party had already booked all the rooms for the next two days.

My journalist friend Golap Batra, the UNI manager, had not yet turned up to receive us and make our room arrangements. Also did I tell the hotel manager that prior information had also been given. He agreed, but pleaded helpless.

'But for the *barat* party?'

Rudely did he say, 'I can't help you.'

'Please consider. Just for our overnight stay. Your *barat* party will come next day before noon. By that time we'll vacate it, as we'll leave for Jaisalmer by the evening train.'

Still he was unrelenting.

Just then Golap arrived and heard the story from me. He then talked to the manager.

A room was then allotted just for the night, and we were told, after breakfast, we would have to move into the lounge for staying until the train time.

Golap departed after saying he would be coming back with a car to show us the palace, the half portion having been converted into a five-star hotel as in Udaipur.

We moved into the allotted room for a wash and to get prepared for the lunch with whatever we got. But to our dismay we found the room could not be bolted from inside. By pushing a chair and a table we shut the door and finished our washing and dressing. After lunch, we locked the room from outside and waited at the lounge for Golap to come.

Golap came; the car, too; and we left for the palace, which from a distance looked pink. We went into the hotel and after spending a few moments we came out to visit his flat where we had tea.

Our detailed plans for Jaisalmer visit were discussed. He told us he had already informed one Mr. Vyas, the public relations manager of the railways there, who would do all that would be necessary.

It was also decided Golap would book a retiring room at Jodhpur station for our stay after our return from the desert journey. Also would he make our reservations for the return trip to Jaipur. I paid him advance money for doing all this.

After our arrival at the Jodhpur station for our onward journey to Jaisalmer we bought tickets. Before we got into the train, we had tea. The sandy town was getting cool. Just at six in the evening the metre-gauge train left for the desert railhead leaving behind the wavy hands of my friend.

The train was whizzing past dark rural clusters. For a few minutes it halted at Pokhran, the site for Indian nuclear tests. Awake though, I did not think of getting down on the platform to have a feel of our national power.

That the desert looks so wonderful at night I did not know. From the window of the running train what was visible was a long spread of the hessian-coloured sand basking in the affection of a pale moon.

Possibly I was sleepy or dozing off swinging with the train movement when the whistle went off with a continued refrain. Peeping out from the window I found the night was fading away into a misty dawn. Out in the open, I felt it would be cold. Away in the distance a sketchy outline of a hillfort emerged. Gradually, the sun rose, its golden hue falling on the fort and turning it to be a captive wonder. Usha got up. She looked out. I told her it was the Sonarkella of the great filmmaker of ours, Satyajit Ray.

PR man Vyas received us at the Jaisalmer station, saying he had already got the message from Golap and booked room for our day-long stay at the PWD bungalow. As desired by him, I purchased our return tickets for Jodhpur. The same train would take us there. It would start at eight in the evening and reach Jodhpur the next morning.

Arriving at the bungalow by jeep, we had breakfast after wash. The jeep had left with Mr. Vyas. He had said he would come back before lunch.

Outside of the rest house, on the road, we saw a camel chewing thorny bushes. Holding its rein the owner was standing. He approached us for a ride. We nodded. The camel then sat on the road peculiarly bending its knees one after another. The owner held me first and I got up; then it was the turn of Usha, who astonishingly made it well and sat behind me, clasping me tight, breathless and putting all her weight on me.

I was praying for the divine energy to stand the weight; fortunately, I discovered my wife was not the last straw on the camel's back.

The lunch over, we came to the office of the district forest officer. He spoke about his experimental efforts at social forestry that was changing the face of the desert. Not all trees grew, some did; 'and they are of smaller varieties on which we are concentrating.' The result? 'Wonderful. Green is growing.'

The officer offered us a jeepride in the heart of the desert to show us the face-lift. We were glad to accept the offer. In the afternoon, when the sun was still shining above our heads, a jeepload of curious persons, journalists and photographers included, left for a roundabout travel on the sand. Rings of forest were eyefuls of surprise and in the middle of a ring there stood one rockbuilt golden temple though in ruins.

For about two hundred kilometres we moved in the Thar seeing snakes, peacocks and hordes of wild camels with blood oozing from their mouths. The camels saw us and suddently disappeared beyond the sandy waves.

We then came to Sam full of dunes, on our way back to Jaisalmer. Climbing down from the jeep, just for fun, we mounted the dunes where our feet sank deep. The sun was then above the low horizon glowing red, our shadows lengthening; and the coming darkness was slightly windy.

A superb moment for meditation! But our divinity within did not allow us to enjoy the blissful moments for long.

Sam is forty kilometres away from Jaisalmer where we would have to reach to catch the train after dinner.

The DFO was in a hurry. Soon, on the way, he saw a man tall and sturdy yet in tatters, walking tired on the metalled road. He stopped our jeep and asked for water in folded hands. The DFO took pity on him, left his seat and brought the bagful of water from under the backward leg space. He poured the water down into the man's hands, but soon he yelled, 'Oh, man! You're drinking like a camel.' The man stopped drinking and rinsed his mouth with his turban.

'Where're you from?'

No answer.

'Where'll you go?'

'Jaisalmer.'

Just one word the man said. The DFO whispered to me, 'Such things are common on this road which runs straight to the Pakistani border.' But I did not understand what he meant by it.

The man then wanted a lift and got it. The DFO was not rude to him. But on reaching Jaisalmer he just went away silently.

It was dark when we came to the rest-bungalow and hurriedly we collected our luggage to leave for Mr. Vyas's residence where we would have the dinner. Before arriving there we bought some sweetmeats from a wayside shop as a token of gratitude to the Vyas family.

Leaving Jaisalmer behind us made me sad. I was in pensive mood, but when I felt the train was moving I got alert. Moving my head out of the window I saw from a distance the Vyas family was standing on the platform waving hands to which I readily responded.

Usha went to sleep on her berth but I kept awake all the night watching eagerly the swiftly passing sands.

And off and on my mind flew into the distant Sam. I wished I remained sitting on the dune deep in meditation for a divine flight to the golden sun. Would I get lost in the fireball? Would it be my divine salvation?

The train was moving. So were my thoughts.

Golap had arranged for our short stay in a retiring room at the Jodhpur station. We had bath and breakfast. And then rest. At Golap's flat we had our lunch. And too much of talking. Late in the afternoon we returned to the retiring room for a catnap.

Just in time we got ready for boarding the night express to Jaipur. Golap gave a hand in spreading our bed rolls on berths. Really, for all practical purposes, Golap means rose, a flower of binding love. We left him on the platform as the train moved, but the aroma of his divine presence remained and travelled with us to the rosy dawn.

11

GOING PLACES (III)

Woman, no cry.

'Yes, Usha, please don't cry. Why should you?'
'No, I must. Don't you see the anguish in my face?'
'But after a good sleep the whole night, I must say you should be bright as the rising sun.'
'I can't. I'm so morose.'
'But why? Don't you hear the tuneful song by Bonnie M?'
'I do, still I can't forget I've missed Bikaner.'
'Ah! This is then your problem. But why don't you think in a journey so big as it were we've to miss many a place though worth seeing?'
'But I won't argue with you now. I'm sad.'
'Why do you forget we've missed so many places during our several visits we've made all over the country?'
'I know'.
'Then? We've missed Kovalam; Ooty, Panchmarhi, Bhopal, Gwalior, Ahmedabad, Baroda, Surat, Porbandar, Dwarka, Kulu, Manali, Ladakh, Deoghar, Rajgir, Mirik, Kalimpong, Sikkim, Bhutan, Tripura, and . . .'
Oh! stop all such audio-nuisance. I'm sick of it. What I'm saying this time we've missed Bikaner – thus spoke Usha, and she was out of breath.
OK. Let me stop talking bosh. Better we should take a move out, or we'll miss the bus - I sounded a bit rude to her, and

holding her in one hand I asked my porter to call a rickshaw for going to the bus-stand.

Woman, no cry.

The Jaipur station area was very crowded even at this morning hour and we had to make our way through the human maze for catching hold of a rickshaw.

The Agra-bound bus was already full, still we could get two seats in the middle. And after getting the accommodation on the bus I did not feel like going to the Bengali manager. Probably, he had not come so early. I asked Usha if she would like to eat something. She gave the nod. Luckily, we finished our mouthwash in the train before it reached Jaipur. Still I took out the water jug and got down from the bus to buy some food for us.

The sun was far above the horizon now, but it was not hot. Our onward journey to Agra had already begun. We were crossing the city limits fast. To our left the skyline had the sunbath, the hills accompanying us being green somewhere but barren and rocky at some places. Far away we had a glimpse of the Amber Palace. seemingly giving us a standing send-off.

Smoothly on the paved road the bus was speeding fast changing the scenario from the hills to the low valley and then to the plains.

Usha had already started dozing off, but I remained sitting erect holding the front-seat rod tightly. I was as usual dumb-found. And silent. Why this was so I cannot explain. I have always found whenever I make a journey the sleep gives me the slip.

Perhaps, several wild thoughts overburden my mind, and this time, too, my mind had gone over to the far-away Aravalli range of hills shadowing the Arabian Sea and its blue waters on the Western Ghats. Thoughts also flashed through my wide-awake mind about how Aravallis were fading into the Sahdara hills, also on the Western Ghats. The long range of the Western Ghats had put a high barrier to the sea breeze turning the other side into a virtual barren tract. Along our bus trip from Ajanta to Jalgaon a roadway cut out of the hills ran almost parallel to the road on the plains. The southernmost tip of the sub-continent had also given us an idea of this vast line of the ridge. The Vivekananda Rock seemed to be the final point at Kanyakumari.

The Eastern, Ghats, too, came to my mind in a flash. From Ranchi to Deoghar there had been a spread-out of Chhotanagpur hilly ranges, and then down south the Nilgiri hills and the Simlipal hills both covered almost the entire areas in Orissa, and further down in Andhra up to Vizag the massive expanse of the soil had been cut up by numerous waves of hills, again blocking the sea breeze from the Bay of Bengal, but because of low pressures in the atmosphere the other side of the Eastern Ghats was not denuded of rainfall.

The Thar developed on the Western Ghats but the Eastern Ghats were not cruel.

And many other thoughts so overwhelmed me that I could not think of anything else than the bare bones of the mundane matter. Divinity within got muddled.

The expansive wall of the Himalayas on the north of the sub-continent stands as a blockade to the icy cold wind from the upper regions extending up to the Arctic, but for which our vast land would have been snowbound excepting the tapering-off shorelines.

Clouds I saw crawling upward in the mountains of the Kashmir Valley; even on the top of the Vaishnodevi hills clouds were seen resting; at Shimla, too, clouds appeared kissing hilltops; from Kausani I could see patchy clouds coming from the west to touch like a tangent the tip of the high Trishul; and at Darjeeling facing the majestic Kanchenjunga clouds climbed the ranges like mountaineers, steadily and skilfully,

Hills dwarfed by snow-capped peaks of the Himalayas were a grandeur. From the Binsar forests the semicircular waves of hills looked awfully splendid. Samlatal and Mayabati, the high places of worship and meditation, were the ideal *ashramas* to feel the divine vibrations of Sri Ramakrishna and Swami Vivekananda; and from these places the monks and householders alike looked in wonder up the northern peaks for imagining if they were making trips through the icy walls to Kailash and Manasarovar, away in Tibet.

On the way to Mayabati we came across a legendary place Devidura where, we were told, the Pandavas had once stayed; and beyond the deep valley there was the Pancholi range where the five wandering brothers used to cook their food. I saw the expansive awe, a divine excellence, the white curves of peaks all basking in bright and blissful sunshine.

It is idiotic for me to claim that I am a divinity incarnate. Not that. But strange things happen. Always. And one or two such out-of-the-ordinary things have occurred in my life for which I can say I have an innate power to learn from boyhood that there is divinity within me as much as in other beings which often propels me to understand the circumstances helping to 'evolve God out of the material man'. With my inner eye I saw the radiant face of Swami Vivekananda, unbelievably smiling at me for such realization.

Is it funny? No. My feelings about Mayabati and Samlatal up in the Pithoragarh hills are genuinely realistic, devoid of any preconception or afterthought. And I can add Almora to these two *ashramas* for correctly unveiling my perception.

So a few more words about these sacred hill-sites would not be irrelevant.

Blessed by the physical presence of Swamiji over a hundred years ago, Mayabati has now become not only a place of pilgrimage but also a divine haven for meditation in sylvan silence. A branch of the Advaita Ashrama of far-down Kolkata spiritually associated with the Ramakrishna and Vivekananda order, the Mayabati centre does not profess idolatry but meditation in a serene surrounding, under the constant watch of the great Himalayas.

Contrarily, Samlatal is the place for devotional worship–day in and day out prayers are offered to the Trinity of Sri Ramakrishna, Srima Sarada and Swami Vivekananda. And the prayer song of *Khandana Bhava* composed by Swamiji reverberates through woods down to the lake and beyond. Similarly, at Almora the same kind of worship is performed as at Samlatal, but with a difference. The glass-covered prayer hall opens up a wide-screen view of the snow-white Lord Shiva the Divine. It was to this epitomised divinity I bowed down in humble obeisance when one day I entered the home of prayer.

Mayabati forests are well preserved with the green abounding all over, but Samlatal presents a sordid picture of barrenness. Especially, around the lake which is now shallow, its banks grassless, with shops mushrooming, its soil fast losing grip and facing erosion, this small hill abode of God may be less charming as days pass by and if the danger to divinity is not stopped at once.

I could not imagine what the government or the Ashrama was thinking of in order to put a brake on such an unbecoming erosion of divinity.

It is true Samlatal has a great tourism potential because of its picturesque elevation and proximity to the border with Nepal. And for this reason the human greed for doing business with beauty has so much increased that all concerned are finding it difficult to fight construction of the tourist complex on the erosion of divine values. I just could stand on the bank of the lake looking at what would be happening to the prayer-place. Would the sublime eco-order be destroyed, and that, too, for some money-spinning?

Wild thoughts made me pensive. Effortlessly, my hand moved near my heart. Did I try to feel if the divinity within me was not disturbed?

I did not know what I was doing, but when the speeding bus gave me a rude jolt while negotiating a bump on the road, I came to my senses.

But all this was diversion for me, for a moment. The road ahead was smooth yet spewing smoke under the bright sun. And again my mental anatomy got disjointed and wild thinking began. I was thinking of the midlands in our peninsula where a number of rivers, some big, some small, flow mostly from the north to the south, or to the seas. Was it for this that India's great civilization is river-linked? The Ganga and Godavari, the Brahmaputra and Narmada, the Yamuna and Saraswati, and the Krishna and Kaveri, all have provided us with riverine tracts, all taken together making a criss-cross pattern of beauty seldom found elsewhere in the world.

In Bengal, which in 1947 split into two parts – East and West, this was the beauty showered on us by bountiful nature. But today?

The bus was approaching our destination Agra, yet there was no full-stop to my wild thoughts.

Santiniketan is in West Bengal while Silaidaha is in the East, but, good luck, Rabindranath still lives in one body. There has been a tortuous tug-of-war over Kazi Nazrul, Kolkata and Dhaka infamonsly warring over his poetic faculties. Rabindranath did not face any challenge from prosaic charlatans while Nazrul did. But today, the air seems to have settled down to damp coolness.

Before I got another big jolt I thought it would have been better if there was a Bengal Wall perpetrating the great divide, but unlike the Berlin Wall the ill-starred separation wall would have remained permanent.

But what is it today? Has the *Souhardya* bus done anything like a drastic demolition of the divide?

Incidentally, Charghat my sweet village appeared in my thoughtful mind. Its attraction is something different, still in my thoughts a simple and modest village where I was born and where people are a homely lot though demographically unused to the newer setting; yet not incorrigibly polluted.

Going places brings about invariably a kind of character revolution. But I cannot shed my humble village from my mind.

And now Agra, where exists the Taj Mahal of divine elevation!

12

EAR-RING ISLANDS (I)

Ever on the move we were, as a wandering couple. We saw hills and plains, valleys and deserts, and forests and rivers. Seldom were we on the high seas, earlier though we had enjoyed one coastal cruise, from Mumbai to Goa. Air travels were few and far between; within the circuitous route from Kolkata to Delhi to Mumbai to Kolkata we made some journeys.

On a pilgrimage to Ganga Sagar once we made a steamer journey down the Hooghly river. We started from Outram Ghat, went down to the *sangam*, took holy dips to satisfy our divine urge, and returned to the city. We prayed to Kapil Muni for being blessed by his divine hand.

Standing wide-eyed at the confluence of the Ganga and the Sagar we thought of going one day beyond the mass of wavy waters and, strangely, the day of sea-voyage came one day. We visited the Andaman and Nicobar Islands.

Far down south of the mainland of India, on the Bay of Bengal, the long stretch of the Andaman and Nicobar Islands dangles like an ear-ring and the strings that hold the islands in place are just imaginary.

From the north the islands go downwards to the south, the Andamans coming up in the north and the Nicobars down in the south.

We had longed for visiting the islands but the right moment was not coming. So when the proposal for the visit was mooted by a close relation of ours the joy knew no bounds. Happiness was irresistibly strong.

But the plans were at first sketchy. Bimal Chakraborty, our relative, just gave us an outline of the plans. We did not lose time in discussing them in detail. The final shape got us offguard. Literally, we were up for the go. Bimal's friends, too, agreed to the outing.

The sea voyage, however, did not come first on the agenda. It materialised afterwards. We decided to take the Kolkata-Port Blair-Kolkata flight and in the meanwhile we would make the sea-trip to the Nicobar islands. To the north in the Andamans we would use car, bus and launch for the tours.

Bimal said he had already talked to his friend at Port Blair for our hotel accommodation there. Other arrangements would be finalised on our arrival at the hotel. Bimal's friend in Kolkata, Badhan Sengupta and Tushar Bag, were all agog with the grand idea of being together in the emerald islands.

On a misty morning of November our team – we were nine, or eight plus, four couples and a teenager daughter – flew out of the Dum Dum airport by a jet plane which soon soared high to kiss the sky and below appeared the mirrored blue. The sea and the land just became a void.

Airborne we spent an hour and fifty minutes during which the breakfast and tea were served. Suddenly we felt our plane was losing the altitude fast. For a moment we got nervous, but seconds later we were told the plane would be landing now at Port Blair. From the window we could see the strips and sprouts of islands in green skirts with wavy sparkles of white frills.

And then the touchdown, a little jerky; and the roaring came to a halt on the rain-washed runway We stepped down and looked at the welcoming green with an unusual awe.

The formalities over, we got into a big car in waiting. Bimal's friend, who was standing by the car, greeted us with folded hands. His humility was so touching that made us feel well at home.

We drove to a hotel Hornbill Nest terraced on a hill by the sea and after room allotments we had tea together. In the lounge was hanging a large map of the islands, the important places dotted with colourful marks. The friend of ours helped by his assistant discussed the entire plan of the tour while gossiping about transport, hotel and sightseeing. Bimal was the captain of our team, he took note of everything of the plan.

Freshened up our team of 'eight plus' made for the famous Corvyn's Cove beach a few coconut groves away, just below the hill. The beach looks like a crescent, sandy at one stretch, rocky at another. And as we were walking, our bare feet were washed by foamy waters.

But whose waters were they from? Obviously, the sea was generous. Yet was it all that I felt within me? Not that. It was something else. Were the waters then the divine bliss I had been seeking? Was the hand of God pouring them on us, as Swami Vivekananda had done to Sister Nivedita? Or was Lord Jesus who had washed the feet of his disciples? No, not that much. At the most I could seek the blessings of the man above man, but such realization that Swamiji or Jesus had been showering blessings was too great to achieve.

Neither could my wild thoughts waken me up to a sorry thinking that the last time had come for my own divine existence. I stood still on the sand feeling the sublime cool at my feet.

Back in the hotel we had our lunch, all good dishes but costly. Sitting idly in the lounge, a little drowsy, yet trying to keep our eyes open by looking at the sea where, it seemed, the burning sun was getting cool, when all of a sudden the car of Bimal's friend came. We moved out for sight-seeing in the city, instead we decided to see the five-points in islands around Port Blair. Boarding a launch we made the rounds ending with visiting the infamous Viper Island full of green foliage but also of the bad odour of long-decomposed criminals who had once been sent to the gallows there.

The bliss of the rising sun we did not have as we were all late in getting up from the soft bed perhaps for the dreams come true in rainbow colours.

But in the same afternoon a flash-message came from Bimal's friend which said that the giant luxury ship Harshabardhan, now anchored at Port Blair, would sail for the Nicobar Islands after two hours. We lost no time in deciding for making a voyage. Dream come true!

Formalities were done quickly. Some necessary permissions were taken from the authorities for visiting the inner circles of protected life. The Nicobarese have their own life-style far short of our realization. They must not be disturbed, even though, unlike some other primitive men and women, they are increasingly joining the mainstream. Yet the prior permission is the best preventive.

We left for the ship but on the way to the harbour we made some delay for which, as we entered the port area, we found the ship was about to leave without us. Anchors had been lifted, the ship was a little adrift, and we were standing at the dock helpless. We waved to the captain, who was standing near the window; he signalled the crew for stopping the ship. He had been watching us and as we were reporting late he sent out the alert.

Hurriedly, a staircase was lowered but the steps were upside down. Even so I went up the steps safe holding the two suitcases tightly, but when Usha was coming up bending low and holding sides the staircase suddenly slipped. There was hue and cry. Usha was about to slip into the gap in between the ship and dock. She was asked to get down quickly or else she would get battered. She was trembling as she got down; and I heard the loud heartbeats of mine. The staircase was then fixed up properly. Usha got up. So followed other members of our team.

Perplexed as I was, instead of looking for the divine bliss within, I looked out of our frontal gap into the sky in frenzied thankfulness.

For us deluxe cabins were booked. We entered and occupied them one after another and made ourselves comfortable inside. But there was no tea. The tea time was over.

The five nights that we spent on the ship were a wonderful time, and the expansive sea remained mostly calm with the dolphins dancing on the waves as playful children of the water-god.

Our first port of call was Car Nicobar, a tiny oval island with shiny shorelines and inviting beaches all over, the inland spread covered with the green foliage of coconut and wood trees.

The ship was anchored midstream, its size preventing it from going to the jetty, for the shore water was shallow.

For the first time during the voyage the heavy winds blowing over the mid-sea met with high waves making the pontoon platform bump and toss. The ship's steward lowered the hydraulic bridge to help the passengers for the island jump safely on to the platform, for being ferried to the jetty. Regular passengers did not have to worry about, but new visitors like us were very nervous.

Tushar jumped to the dancing pontoon followed by wife Rita and daughter; Badhan took the next jump hauling down wife Sabita. I came down with much effort but Usha far behind was standing unmoved on the bridge. Bimal was coaxing wife Sima to move along with Usha. In vain. Then Bimal jumped into the float but could not convince Usha and Sima to follow him. Both, afterwards, toiled hard to learn the acrobatic feat. Ultimately, they made it. We waited for a few minutes for the ferry to come, our dances gaining sublime heights yet without any divine bliss.

Bimal's friend Yusuf Bhai, a top businessman of Car Nicobar and other adjoining islands, had sent a car to pick us up from the jetty. We got into it and soon reached his office and were offered seats.

Yusuf Jadwet, his full name, hails from Surat in Gujarat and has built up a business empire in the Bay islands. He welcomed us with a broad smile at the gate.

We were in a hurry, as we would have to return to the ship by four in the afternoon. So we did not waste time. He asked his driver to make the trip round the island.

Our first stop was at the Breaker's Point where a new large jetty was coming up for accommodating big ships. The jetty was fast taking shape while berths were yet to be built up. Boulders had been strewn all over covering spaces along the nice beach playing a sun-and-shadow game under leaning coconut trees. And the breakers lashed the boulders with sprinkles of rainbow-coloured drops of water creating a mystic haze of romanticism sublimating the blue behind. A little later we came to the Shore Beach. It was so hot out there that we got sun-burnt, yet our womenfolk braved the blaze and collected untiringly some artworks of the sea including oysters and shells.

Then we took the road to shadows. To our amazement we saw rows of coconut trees bending low, their heads meeting, as if they were giving us a welcome salute.

At a shaded retreat of Yusuf Bhai we had plenty of green coconut water which quenched our thirsts and soothed our nerves.

A few minutes' drive and we found a church repaired and refurbished. The church had been destroyed by the Japanese during the Second World War. And several clergymen were then massacred whose names came in plaques. Sad and sombre I asked myself why war merceneries were so cruel. Was religion their enemy? War-maniacs could not be divine, but why?

The sun went behind us. We were proceeding along the arch-type shoreline adorned by swaying coconut trees and came across a bunker created by war-mongers but now turned into a viewpoint of beauty and love. I alighted from the car and entered into it with my head low yet touched by the worn-out thatched roof. Was it a prayer for no-war divinity?

We passed by a school where we found teenage boys and girls playing together till then and small children were on their way home, everybody quite unconcerned about the horried past. Will their future be romantic, smiling with the times, in the mainstream of life divine? I had this question in my mind and the answer possibly was waiting in the wings.

Twin wonders of Car Nicobar greeted us on the way. One wonder was the Nicobarese hut that looked like a war-helmet while the other wonder was a three-headed coconut tree. Barefooted we entered one such big hut, virtually a prayer hall full of panels of Christian clergymen. Around it were scattered several huts where the Nicobarese live. I met an old man sitting on a bench at the basement built on coconut-tree plinths and fully uncovered, so made to keep the air cool by letting in the sea-breeze, and if there was high tide the sea water would then only flood the basement without damaging the hut. And about the quaint coconut tree the story goes originally it had four heads all emerging from the same trunk in the middle, but later one head had fallen off.

After over fifty kilometres of the circuitous tour our car seemed to get tired and entered the compound of Yusuf Bhai's residence for rest. We got down and looked for the host. In the drawing room we sat on sofas reclining. The TV was on. We watched a cricket match. Then the host appeared without the hostess. We were told she had gone to Port Blair.

Our lunch was arranged in a big hall adjoining his residence. A young Bengali employee of his supervised our 'eating exercise' as we were so hungry.

It was time for our departure. The car brought us to the office of Yusuf Bhai.

'Thank you. Bye.'

'Same to you.'

The jetty was nearby. We reached it by car in a moment. A launch was waiting for us. It cut through the low waves. We then stood on the float, still dancing, and when the hydraulic bridge was lowered to lift us, we once again went through the acrobatic feats.

It was just the tea time.

The ship moved, towards the south, further down to the tip of the Nicobar Islands almost near the point where the bay meets the Indian Ocean. After dinner, Usha went into the cabin and me to the deck, a few passengers sitting or standing under the star-lit sky. And to the sides of the ship, the vast sea lay with lighter waves on and the indistinct horizon yonder.

Late as I was in getting up I could not see the sun rising from the ocean depth, but the morning was bright which enabled me to see the Great Nicobar on the right lying silent like a stupendous whale. The entire stretch of the long island looked green though draped frugally in greyish clouds. The ship turned near the island and was coasting along. Our destination was Campbell Bay, the southernmost port of call. A ship officer told us to buy return tickets there at the Campbell Bay office after we disembarked.

It was about lunch-time when Campbell Bay came and the ship was anchored midstream, away from the harbour. The exit passage of the ship was crowded, the door opened and the hydraulic bridge lowered, but the pontoon float tugged to a launch stood far away. When it would start moving to the ship few could say. In the meantime we had our lunch.

About three in the afternoon, with the sun-heat a little mellowed, we watched the launch was moving to the ship hauling the float, which appeared bigger than the earlier one at Car Nicobar.

When the puller-launch came near the ship it was late afternoon with the sun just above the hilly range on the wastern sky. We were afraid we would not be able to see the Campbell Bay port town by taking time to move freely. We had been alerted by the ship officer that there was only one tugging back to the ship and we would have to avail of it or we would be stranded as the ship would steam off to the north.

'Without us?'

'Sorry; it can't be helped. We've our schedule'.

'Then we'll not have time to see the town and move to the Indira Point, the southernmost tip where large tortoises swim from Australia to lay eggs on the shore at the point.'

'But even if you had time you can't proceed to the point as it is about forty-five kilometres away. You can at the most cover thirty or thirty-five kilometres by bus or car and after that the road is cracked and damaged, not yet repaired. So you'll have to walk up to the shore.'

So we gave up the wild idea of going to the Indira Point, but hoped at least a few areas of the port town could be seen.

Bimal had earlier sent the message of our intended visit to his friend Chadda, a transport businessman from Punjab now settled at Campbell Bay. On the jetty Chadda Bhai was waiting to receive us. We saw him waving his hand. Our float was on the move and we remained standing as it was crowded.

The breeze on the jetty cheered us but for a moment only, for the information Chadda gave us dampened our spirit. We were bewildered about what to do. He said his car was in the garage undergoing some urgent repair. Then? 'Don't worry. I've the truck, kept ready for you.' He showed us the omnivehicle standing by on the edge of the jetty and said convincingly, 'You're nine. So there'll be no problem in getting room for you all in it.'

I looked at my watch and found there was little time for our detour on the land. Bimal decided to buy return tickets at first. We left for the port office, a little distance away, up the hill.

Bimal and Tushar got down from the truck and went to the office for buying tickets. Time ticked by, and there was no sign of them for long. We were waiting, all hungry for tea and snacks. But where was to get them? I was looking around and saw a bus wending its way on the other side of the creek. The sun had already made its exit behind the range, it was getting dark. Tensions mounted. A guava tree was located nearby, and our Sikh driver took pity on us and went down to pluck some ripe fruits for us. Thankfully, we received them and started munching them with pleasure. The guavas were really juicy.

Bimal and Tushar returned to the truck with tickets in hand, smiling. But it was better if we had tea, just that. A tea stall we could see on the way back to jetty, but we did not stop as we were already late in boarding the pontoon for our water-trip back to the ship. I got exhausted and angry. 'We don't need tea, let's move to the jetty.' Back in the jetty Bimal made a request to Chadda for arranging tea for us. His friend sent a man to the shore but he came back with only snacks and soft drinks. What an irony of fate! Divinity eluded us.

It was dark, jetty lights had been switched on, and the entire scenario looked like a fairyland, yet dog-tired with headache, I could not enjoy the sight. My divinity was miserly, too hidden down under my limbs to come out with its flowering bliss. While moving down the surfing waves I saw the lights of the ship all glaring and possibly for that reason the blinking lights of distant Sumatra could not be seen.

The pontoon was full. It took much time to jump on to the hydraulic bridge for our entry into the shiphold. I went straight into my cabin telling Usha that I would not take any food. While lying down on my bed I felt the ship had been moving northward, leaving behind us the port town of Campbell Bay and our land of disappointment. The night passed off peacefully.

The next day, after lunch, the ship touched the shore of Nancowrie, which island we would visit as we had the necessary permission.

Looking at the cloudy sky we were afraid it might rain at any moment. Still we decided to go ashore. A ship officer had told me there was a queen's palace in the island but he could not say if the queen was in.

Luck favoured us this time as a double-deck launch ferried us to the shore. So we could avoid the jumping gym. But what was frightening us was the rain might ruin our trip to the lady of the island. But no, the cloud just disappeared. It was so kind.

Ashore we had to wait for further army go-ahead for which there was some delay in reaching the palace of the island queen. A guide came with us. We followed him. A narrow metalled road led us to a wooden hut. The guide told us, 'This is the house.'

'Is it?' We said. He answered it was.

The palace, if at all, was nicely built and the decorations within were so awe-inspiring. Unbelievable. A humble and modest cottage could be a palace, how?

The guide informed us the queen was away in Delhi and her daughter the princess had gone to Port Blair.

At first, we were hesitant. The guide said, 'Never mind. Come in. Make yourselves comfortable.'

Upstairs we went and sat in a well-decorated room, its walls flooded with photographs showing the queen and family with Mrs. Indira Gandhi. In albums we saw some pictures of the queen with Rajiv Gandhi when he had visited the green island as Prime Minster.

While having tea with snacks the guide informed me about the property of the queen duly preserved by the government.

On our return walk to the double-deck launch we met some girl students of a local school. They were looking at us in wonder, some smiling, some giggling.

The ship was sailing north, past the islands on the right, then lost into the darkness. The deck had the lights on; we sat and gossiped. For long, with the crew of the ship joining us in the chorus of togetherness. Then we retired.

On the eve of Diwali, and it was late in the afternoon, the ship was anchored off Car Nicobar. Nobody was allowed to get down. On the deck where darkness was gradually descending we stood, all talking shop and some looking at the sun which was setting behind the dark-lined woods of the island.

Within seconds the sun went down but suddenly there appeared on the horizon cloudy graphics illumined red. The graphics remained fascinating and fantastic for a few awful moments. Cracker bursts were heard from the island, some fireworks went up with sprinkles of bulbs falling on the groves.

The ship would sail into Port Blair on the morning of the day of the festival of light. Kali Puja would be held at night in the city, a thousand miles away from our city of Kolkata. We were away from home. Sad.

But we did not know then the evening would not be a sad occasion.

Back in Port Blair we put up in a terrace hotel — Megapode, as arranged by Bimal's friend for being near to the central place from where tour programmes could easily be prepared and movements hurriedly made.

Resting a while after lunch, I rang up a relation of mine, Pinaki Roy, an engineer who had settled in the Andamans and was doing good business. His residence is on a road which runs parallel to the airport runway, and I got the phone number from his mother-in-law who happens to be a cousin sister of my wife. Pinaki's wife Piku on receiving the phone sent her daughter Muniya and two cars to pick us up from our hotel. Muniya, a grown-up girl then doing her graduation away in Goa, faced me on the corridor with a smile, and we all got into the cars for the lift. Pinaki and Piku were at the gate to receive us.

But before our arrival at Pinaki's residence Muniya made a detour of the undulating city to show us Goddess Kali at the temple built by Bengali evacuees years ago. *Puja* arrangements were under way, some Bengalis were dancing to the beating of drums, and we had *prasadam* in packets. From there we went to the Ramakrishna Mission where *sadhus, brahmacharis* and *ashrama* boys were giving final touches to the worship.

Diwali lights all over the Port spreading like strings of garlands mixed with sounds of cracker bursts were enough to produce an ethereal atmosphere of the manifestations of the all-pervasive divinity, my own inner feeling becoming an appendage to all that was great.

The dinner, gossip and affection over, we returned to the hotel for the night. The morning after, our programmes would begin with visits to past memories in the Ross islands. The memories of the colonial thumb-rule, their remnants being too tearful to be eye-opening, betrayed our abject servitude to the whips of misfortune, although centuries later, one day, a subdued nation woke up to a divine realization of self-rule. Even then the treasures of the island have become tourist wonders and the government today is preserving them as they were though in ruins. We walked around looking at the ruins, everything awful—the printing press, the swimming pool, its high wall being lashed by sea waves, the faded-out church with its wall and ceiling decorations remaining intact in coloured lines, all of beauty, the hospital complex, just a fossilised skeleton, all devoted works of the master builders of the bygone days. We roamed about. We fed the deer, too. Then, rest; and the return launch came for journey back to the shore.

At Jolly Buoy we had deep look into the under-sea wonders, the corals of varied hues flowering scattered, and as I was circling in the boat peeping through the fibre glass fitted at the bottom of the boat I honestly felt my psycho-physio elements had all been blessed beyond comprehension. It was the divine supreme that had enveloped me from head to feet.

Besides corals, the miracles like shells, shellfishes, small octopuses and snakes came to my view. Usha missed a red coral. Standing on the sand I saw some tourists diving deep and some by snorkelling. Bimal, Badhan and Tushar with their familes floated on the water with glass-fitted eyes kept open for viewing the corals.

With the lunch packets in hand we walked the distance to the mangrove forests to enjoy food. Wild trees guarded us from the scorching sun and ruffling wind.

Some foreigners, tanned and in bikinis, were swimming with snorkels, but we did not understand they were being watched by guards. When one white woman came out of the water with a living conchshell in hand, she was caught and the creature seized and thrown back into the water. Smilingly the guard said, 'You can take home some bits and pieces of memory.'

13

EAR-RING ISLANDS (II)

Our tight-scheduled tour programme left us little time for another round of sight-seeing at Port Blair. We had much earlier decided to go northward for seeing the top string of ear-ring islands. And then, after coming back from our northern trip, we would settle down at the port city and visit the remaining places of tourist interest.

But it did not mean the great historic Cellular jail of Port Blair just off the Ross Island was the place of secondary interest. It was a must on our agenda, but as we were short of time and had made bus and hotel reservations already, we had better skip it for the time being.

Still I sounded a warning : The past is a part of history. We can't ignore it, even though visiting the jail of torture would leave in our mouths a bitter taste of unwholesome cruelty.

My other friends said : We enjoy a free life now fully different from the foul past, yet it'll be our folly to bypass a recap of hoary days.

'Thanks. Don't forget it.'

Bimal's friend had prepared our itinerary while we were cruising in the sea. In the meanwhile, we had shifted to another hotel near the bus-stand and the hotel had a pick-up van of its own. So it would not be a problem for us to catch the early morning bus bound for Rangat, our next halt before Mayabunder, the tip of middle Andamans.

The bus was wending its way through forests inhabited by the

Jarwas, the most hostile among the aborigines of the islands. The other tribes who were yet to be tamed are the Andamanese, Shompens, Onges, Sentinelese and the Nicobarese. Besides the Jarwas, the Sentinelese were still inimical. The Nicobarese are in the mainstream while the Onges are on the way to reformation.

Whatever the publicity these few out-of-the-world people get, the fact is they live in deep forests and are well protected from any kind of invasion of their privacy. We could not see the Jarwas; we could not see some other tribes who are still hostile to nature-foes like us. Are they then nature-friendly, the philosophers of all ages? We do not know, as we did not have any idea about their lifestyles.

Some docu-films we were shown by the governmental agencies of the islands, but to my mind they seemed as though they had been made that way. Totally isolated as they are, these old tribals would in the course of time be extinct. The Jarwas, in particular, are on the verge of fading out of existence.

The bus suddenly developed a trouble midway in the forests. It stopped. The driver got down followed by the conductor. The police escort, too, alighted holding his rifle tight. During this forest trek the police remain on guard.

Passengers began to get down from the bus when the driver said the repair work would take time. It was past mid-day. I also moved away from the seat, got down and stood on the road by the side of the policeman. The road was cut out of the hills and well-paved, flanked by tall trees grown on hills.

Coming near the escort I smiled and asked him if we were being watched by the Jarwas. He returned the smile and said, 'How can I say that? But if a poisoned arrow drops nearby, we should be on the alert. They may be warning us.'

I looked around. Fearfully. But behind the trees I found no trace of any hostile element.

The escort said, 'Last year, during the Holi, they attacked a stranded bus and looted the red garments.'

'They love red?'

'Yes.'

The bus was ready. The driver took his seat. The conductor asked the passengers still loitering on the road to get in and take seats. All done, the bus left.

On the way we had to cross two river-creeks with the bus berthed inside for once and in another case we left the bus behind and got into a second bus waiting for us on the bank. This second bus drove us to Rangat, a nice small hill station full of green, the shoreline on the east kissed by the sea.

At the bus stand where we got down Bimal and Tushar inquired at a wayside teastall about the location of our hotel. Somebody said it would be futher up in the hill. A car was available. Along with our women members Bimal went uphill. We waited and then had tea with biscuits. A few minutes afterwards, the car returned with everybody inside. To our wonder, we learnt our hotel was still twenty kilometres away, further north, on the way to Mayabunder.

We would have to go there, but how? Would there be any other car available? The driver informed us there was another car, he could procure that if we wanted. We did want it and he went away and soon came back with the second car.

We were all hungry. At the roadside restaurant we had our fill. We then departed for the reserved hotel, which local people said was newly built facing the sea. As our cars were passing some hilly *ghats* smoothly, I was engrossed in the thoughts the divinity within had in fact been discovered which now was showing us the way to comforts by removing the hazards and tensions of the trip.

Sun-up, and we started: sun-down, and we were still moving on the wheels.

Still I had complete faith in my character of being divine. Spirit would not die.

The entire stretch of our journey was a bliss with the hills and trees rising high on the left hiding the setting sun but the sea on the sloping right looked still blue and still lashing the running beach in white sparkles. Soon afterwards, we entered the hotel compound, the Cuthbest Bay beach, just behind the fishermen's cottages.

The manager, quite young in age, came out all smiles and inquired about our delay. We narrated the full story of our predicament. Rooms were allotted, we got in and until dinner spent our time in gosip.

The morning after was bright, and so it was after my sleep was sound without dreamy hazards. But I could not guess the sunny start would be so short-lived. Whoever said the morning shows the day was wrong; the next few hours might prove to be a nuisance with unimaginable worries and woes sweeping us off the feet. We had better wait for the evening to come to say the day was good.

But it so happened to me and others as well. For a few hours after boarding a crowded bus bound for the next halt at Mayabunder, a port town neatly etched out from the sea with small islands scattered all around emitting an essence of superlative beauty spreading along the green and blue. But I did not know earlier about this heavenly bliss while I was on board the bus bursting at the seams. For me especially the bus trip was an ordeal too unbearable to take in infinite pains. I remained standing without elbow room, my feet up from the landing frame. All my prayers to God went in vain, and when I got a chance to sit after a few kilometres' drive, near a hospital, a young boy, of my grandson's age, just held me back for allowing a young girl, maybe his friend, to sit by him. My God, I must thank you for your ridiculous 'un-divine' act!

My friend Tushar, who had managed to get a seat for him at the rear of the bus, must have noticed my predicament. I was feeling unwell, about to faint, when I had the helping hand from him. He drew me near him, and himself standing up made me seated in his. It was the divine grace, certainly!

After alighting from the bus at about eleven forenoon, I just could tell Bimal, 'We shouldn't have taken the bus. It was the hell of a journey we've had so far.'

Bimal said, 'We've been misled by the conductor. And, more, its earlier bus had a breakdown, so withdrawn. I heard all this in the bus.'

'We could have hired the deluxe coach from the hotel. The manager said so.'

'Yes, that could've been done. But I didn't understand it would be so like.'

Just in front of the tourist lodge where we would put up the bus stopped and we got down bag and baggage, me totally shattered not even having the strength to stand. Usha, too, remained all the time standing, but she did not look worn-out as she had got a ledge to ease her legs.

We went in. It was a spacious lodge with much of green in several open-air compounds, the greyish sea casting its graceful look at it, the tree leaves moving in joy.

But again our luck betrayed us. We were told by the overriding manager that we had been provided with two rooms only, and not four as we had requested.

'In spite of our early booking?'

'Yes.'

'But how can that be?'

'I'm trying, at least for another. Now you take rest at the lounge. The breakfast time is over, still you can have buttered toasts and eggs.'

Again, bag and baggage, we entered the lounge. It was spacious. Tired, we relaxed in sofas. I felt drowsy.

The breakfast was good. We got some energy. Except Badhan and myself all went out to see and enjoy. To my surprise, I saw Usha was sleeping with her head bending low. I did not feel like waking her up. Let her relax in her own way.

For over two hours we were kept waiting at the lounge. And soon we were disappointed. We decided to enter the rooms; as allotted. In the first room I went, but Usha did not. She preferred the second room, and surprisingly it was a better room. Tea came which I took and relaxed in the worn-out couch; but I was alone in my room while the seven plus crowded the other room sipping tea together.

After tea, I gatecrashed into the second room where my companions were all smiles. I was grave and asked them about the lunch. Bimal smilingly said, 'Lunch is not yet ready. They'll call us.'

'All right, but then one point—will I stay alone in that condemned room?'

Bimal was surprised. 'Is that so?'

We finished our wash, and only then the call came from the dining hall. We trooped in.

It was very late in the afternoon. The sun had already hidden his glowing face behind the woods of the rest house. We did not feel like going back into our rooms; we sat on the lawn and went down the steps into the 'northern' Indira Point to enjoy the cool.

Only Bimal was missing; he was possibly greasing the palm of the manager while pleading for another room.

After a few minutes we took the steps up and at the edge we met Bimal. He looked glad and said,'Another room I'll get after the last bus comes from Port Blair.'

'Let's hope so.' We said in a chorus.

The canteen boy called us to the dining hall. Tea was ready. After tea, we moved on to the jetty down the road. It was a long jetty spread from south to north. High waves were battering it. Berthed launches were dancing. We found some anglers busy with their rods.

The jetty, though long, could not berth big ships. Only the inter-island ships or launches came and got anchored for some time or for the night.

Beyond the water horizon the sun went down leaving behind its glow for seconds. The jetty got dark. Lights were on. And we walked up the road to the rest home.

The following morning we saw in wonder a big passenger ship Nicobar anchored mid-sea and passengers were being ferried to it. The ship was Kolkata-bound.

A few islands away to the north of Mayabunder, in the north Andamans, there stands the charming town of Diglipur skirted by hills of which the Saddle Peak is the highest. And clouds climb the peak shading the sun in the background. The Bengalee evacuees from the mainland have made Diglipur their principal habitat.

Our plans originally were to visit Diglipur through Kalighat in the creek where generally the launches ferry passengers. From the small jetty a road has gone up and down to Diglipur, a distance of over twenty kilometres. If a jeep is available one can go and return within hours, but there is hardly available any late afternoon ferry to Mayabunder. And spending the night either at Diglipur or at Kalighat would be hazardous if there are no early reservations in guest-houses. The risk factor is one too many. Few have the luck. We were nine, and without accommodation we would be in a tight spot. So, while coming back to the hotel for tea, we decided to skip

Diglipur and take only the launch which would leave the Mayabunder jetty next morning at nine for Kalighat.

After dinner, a third room was arranged for us to which Bimal and Sima shifted. Would I be wrong if I said divinity had showered its blessings on them? And among the rest of the team Badhan and Sabita, and Tushar, Rita and daughter stayed in the second room, while Usha had come to the original mine.

All the night Usha and me remained wide awake just to kill the legion of mosquitoes always entering our nets full of potholes and openings, and fed up at last Usha folded up the nets for the night. Sleepless and exhausted, we took up in the morning the first job of mending our nets with the thread and stitch. Fortunately, before the breakfast time the hazardous job was done. Would the divine bliss be extended to us at night?

To catch the northward morning launch we hurried to the jetty. Much earlier, Bimal and Tushar had gone to the marketplace for buying tickets with reservation in the private deluxe bus which was due to leave Mayabunder in the following morning at 5.30. It was arranged the bus would lift us from the gate of our rest lodge.

The northward launch left the jetty at 9 sharp fully crowded. We did not get room inside the cabins, so we moved to the front up on the deck and sat in the sun burning overhead though the sea was windy. The launch was dancing on the waves and it was immense joy when we noticed more than a dozen dolphins were accompanying us in a playful mood.

And we were happy to find on the deck several Bengalees either going to Kalighat or Diglipur. They were mostly speaking in Hindi, not in Bengali. It appeared Hindi is the link language in the islands. We had noticed even Tamil-Telugu-Malayalam people at Port Blair speak Hindi fluently.

One Bengalee youth told me, 'Here in the creek under mangroves you can find several crocodiles. We often hunt them. Which earns us a lot of money.'

I replied, 'But where are they? I don't find anyone.' His eyes moved around, but there was none. It was ebb time though.

The ferryboat journey ended: We were at the Kalighat jetty.

The launch came to a halt. The serang told us to return to the boat at noon. It was 10 then.

A landmark in the lower tip of north Andamans, with a hill-wall going up high and the road below zigzagging into oblivion, Kalighat to the Bengalees is a familiar name reminding them of the Kalighat temple of Kolkata. Just across the road a makeshift temple was built; inside was there an image of the goddess. We offered our *pranams*.

I walked up and down the road and saw a daily bazar humming with haggling for fish and vegetables. Yonder I found one or two elephants moving cut timbers and logs with their large trunks into the creeks for towing them into Mayabunder.

But for bad luck or good, we did not see any bus coming either way nor any jeep. Till mid-day we were there loitering on the road; we did not have any chance to 'miss' the bus. The serang, who took meals with us, warned us about the departure time. The hotel was run by a Bengalee who did not encourage us into going to Diglipur since we would not get any evening transport back to Mayabunder.

Diglipur remained our Yarrow Unvisited, a dream that would never come true. Our salutation we gave in grief to Monoranjan Bhakta, M.P, under whose leadership the Bengal evacuees had come and settled mainly in the north Andamans.

The serang then blew the horn. He was calling passengers to board the launch. It was time for departure. Before stepping on to the deck I just took a look at the idol of Kali. I felt my divine yearning got a jolt.

Some of us sat outside with towels on the head yet facing the sun. Myself and Usha preferred to sit inside the cabin avoiding the sunlight.

It was tide. The creek was full. Mangroves were half submerged, the sea-water engulfing wider areas underneath. The small islands ended; and creeks flowed into the sea with high tides struck by winds splashing the entire boat. We got wet, a soothing wet. At times the ferry was tilted by blasting winds, so dangerously that we got afraid. The serang went all over with a smile and said, 'Don't worry.' Tightlipped we sat. A new experience!

Far away, Mayabunder came into my view from the open window. It looked like a tiny tip! Afterwards, I noticed the shaded Indira Point, so-called, a shed built by son Rajiv in mother Indira's memory, under the stony wall of our hotel. The story was Mrs. Gandhi liked the place very much.

From the sun-burnt jetty we walked up the road to the tree-shed of the lodge. Our room being uncomfortable we both preferred to stay out, and then downstepped into the wet of the Indira 'memorial'.

Gradually we found the other members of our batch coming down and sitting by us.

We had tea in the dining hall, me holding the cup in my hand and looking out into far-off islands turned brown by the setting sun.

The compound was dark yet lighted as we entered into our room. After wash, we decided for a round of hot tea. And then, for pack-up. We were almost ready for the next day's bus journey to Port Blair.

We assembled at the lounge and gossiped. The cook then called us in and, as we sat, served good dishes specially prepared for us. The dinner was over, the cook had tips and said 'bye' with a smile.

Our night stay in the same old room was fortunately not the repetition of the previous night's ordeal. Usha had mended the nets repelling the mosquitoes effectively. Our sleep was undisturbed, thanks to Usha. Or was it a kind of divine bliss?

Right on dot the morning bus arrived at the gate of our hotel where we were standing ready to get into it.

Usha sat by the window, me next. The bus sped off. Out I looked, the sun was rising, perhaps beyond the sea, hidden from the eye by tall trees atop a low hill.

From the other window I saw rain-washed green paddy fields extending up to a treeline. The vast paddy fields are a rare sight in the undulating terrain of the Andamans. I was happy to think the divinity within people of this region is blissful.

The bus was moving slow on the wet road with tall trees flanking it. It had rained, the air was damp. Suddenly the bus stopped. It was a minor trouble. Some of our passengers got down. I also came down from my seat to see how the environ looked like. And

I found a bridge ahead and underneath a creek was flowing, the waters being shallow.

The river-creeks further ahead we crossed sitting in the bus placed inside the mouth of the steamers. But thereafter we entered the Jarwa forests and I told Usha we were now moving along alien lands. Usha only opened her eyes and then closed them without concern. There was total peace with the rude sun alone running with us. My divinity within appeared happy.

Now was the time for tea. The Jarwas were far behind. Our bus stopped. The driver alighted. We followed. All our eight plus had tea and snacks. We asked for rice and curry. In vain. *Chapatis* and coconut waters inside the shells would do. We enjoyed them, really.

The bus resumed its journey on a less uneven road, although the sun was unkind. And late in the afternoon we reached the bus-stand. Getting down from the bus bag and baggage we relaxed on the concrete bench looking for the car of Bimal's friend. The car came and we drove to the friend's office to discuss over cups of tea the matters relating to our next programme. We learnt for our overnight stay a luxury guest-house had been arranged at the Chidiya Tappu bird sanctuary some thirty miles away to the west.

The car moved. On the way, from the nearby market, we purchased bagfuls of necessities for the dinner, tea and breakfast. At 10 in the following morning a bus would come up to the guest-house and we would avail of the pick-up from there to the Port Blair terminus. Then we would put up at the Teal House, an old hotel built on the slopes of the hill sliding to the foot of the mini harbour from where small ships and launches and fish trawlers leave.

The Chidiya Tappu guest-house was roomy, its interior decor looking that of film studios, and the facade overlooking the sea with a black barren hill away as though afloat. Our room was in the middle, hedged by Bimal's and Badhan-Tushar's. After bath, we had tea and snacks and out we came for a walk on the lawn in the front. The grass was velvet-soft; up in the sky a dull half-moon was hanging, the calm sea mirroring the creamy light.

An early dinner we had, as we were all feeling too tired to spend time in idle gossips. We jumped on to the bed and lolled on it before sleeping deep. The sanctuary was quiet, so were we.

Early next morning, after tea, we got ready for taking a walk up to a nearby beach. We moved out. Forest trees were drenched, rain-waters falling in drops. The sun was up, yet the road that was moving up and down was wet. Only the birds were not chirping as they did usually.

On the meandering road we were walking in groups seldom talking to feel the music of silence, when a sudden crippling pain gripped Rita, and we found Tushar was holding her fast. We stopped. Everybody thought I was the victim since I had an injured leg pained by arthritis. But it was not so, as I was not immobilised. I looked back and saw Rita shaking and sweating. Rita shouted, 'I can't make it' I hurried to them though limping. I held Rita's hand and told Tushar, 'You better go. I'm taking Rita back to the guest-house.' Usha said, 'That's better. You needn't go to the beach which is still far away.'

Soon the forward party got lost in the wilderness, but we two proceeded slowly back to the guest-house. Rita now was feeling better; me, too. Suddenly she shouted and drew my attention to a big snake crawling into a wayside bush. We halted with a jolt. The snake disappeared. Only then the birds chirped in fear.

On the verandah of the guest-house Bahadur brought out two chairs for us to sit on. I ordered tea for both. While taking sips I thought my morning was not divinely blissful. Yet should I thank God for not inflicting further injury to my leg? Yes, I should, I couldn't make it. Like Rita. Silently I took sips.

Away in the sea I saw only one kite was flying low in circles. Two fishermen, in ankle-deep waters, were then spreading their net to catch fish. All in vain, and the kite flew away.

Our teammates returned after seeing the beach. Usha told me, 'It was good you didn't go. The beach was a long way off.'

'Good beach?'

'Yes.'

Our breakfast was ready We had it. The bus for Port Blair would be coming soon. We packed up.

The bus arrived. Passengers got down. Bahadur helped us board the vehicle and keep the luggage in proper place. Tips in hand, Bahadur went away. His two bright children waved their hands and saw us off.

An hour later we were in a government hotel, Teal House. In our room I opened a window facing the sea and I noticed a large ship moving to the wharf.

Returning from the north we had a short break during which we went places in and around the port city. We saw the mini zoo where we were struck dumb by seeing one jumbo crocodile and his mate both supplying the zoo with so many children who were kept apart in separate enclosures. The birds were all of island varieties – the megapode, the teal and the hornbill, among others.

Trees and timbers of different varieties crowd another museum. Three or more types of timber were made into a semi-tall tree which adorned the gate. It was a novel idea of ornamentation.

Another museum full of exhibits of the land and its aborigines and also of undersea world charms was a place to see with wondrous eyes. The life of the aborigines was a big draw but the life of the corals stole the thunder.

One morning we planned to make a car trip to Mount Harriet, the highest hill in the south Andamans just across the Haddoo harbour having the longest jetty where large ships are berthed. We were told the highest peak in the south would bless the viewers with a panoramic view of Port Blair and its surroundings. But there was a warning — that the hill grasses are full of leeches which move secretively to suck human blood to their hearts' content. Atop we went prepared, taking the lunch packs. We enjoyed the enchanting view of the scattered islands and when we were taking our food we felt the leeches had already made some of us their poor victims. We got alarmed and got rid of the blood-suckers by spreading salt on them.

Also we saw the Sippighat farm run by the government research institute. Nearby there was a rubber plantation area. A Bengalee is the owner. We could not meet him as he was away in Kolkata. Twice we visited the Chatham Saw Mill, a government undertaking, one of the biggest in Asia. And just on the other side of the creek we visited a plywood mill run by a private agency.

In this island city of Port Blair an economy of mutual combination has been so neatly achieved that there occurs hardly any acrimony between two horizontal parts, one run by the government and the other by a private firm. Both are independent and inter-dependent as well, one producing timber and the other plywood, one related to the other in the ultimate analysis of the economy.

What is banned recently in the islands is felling of trees by private predators, yet clandestine deforestation was allegedly going on, as we were told by the concerned people in confidence.

A number of silly questions disturbed me. Unnecessarily? There was no answer. But the questions appeared to me too obsessive to ignore. If life is destined to be divine, what then is the meaning of destroying the treasures of nature and man, the creations of combination?

Is it not all a hoax?

Still divinity seemed to be smiling on us one sunny morning when Bimal stepped into our room to convey a message so long waitlisted. He said, 'Arrangements had been made for the trip to the Havelock Islands, about forty kilometres off in the Andaman Sea.' We, enlivened by the news, danced and sang. 'The Radhanagar beach at Havelock is so beautiful that it draws people from far and near.'

Bimal further said, 'We'll go by the mid-sized ship Ramanujam. Bookings have been made. All cabin seats by the window. Even hotel reservations are complete.'

'One-day trip?'

'No, for one night's stay Tomorrow, early in the day, we're leaving the port; it'll take two hours and a half to reach the island. After reporting at the hotel, we'll spend our time playing with waves on the beach. There's another beach, Shyamnagar. In the afternoon we'll visit that, too. And the day after, the ship journey home.'

But the smile we had on our lips did not last long, since past mid-day the weather worsened so badly that we got alarmed. Bimal sat pressing his mini radio to his ears just to know what would be the forecast. By the sun-down the wind turned into a storm and then into a monstrous cyclone.

In the morning the blast ebbed. With kitbags slinging from our shoulders we came out of the hotel and got taxis for transport to the harbour. Soon we were at the wet jetty.

Whirling clouds were moving so violently towards the west that the ship got the battering most of the time. The rage of the storm increased. The captain was in two minds. And the journey might have to be put off. But nothing such happened. The ship started moving. The voyage was on. But the sea was getting rough more and more. The ship had started rolling up and down. Most passengers started vomitting, some lying down on the floor almost unconscious.

The battered ship could not move an inch forward, but soon afterwards, ironically, it appeared to be moving backward. A voice blared out : We're going back to Port Blair.

Sickness gone, all passengers got up and sighed relief.

A Bengalee marine engineer who was passing by said the ship could cover only seven miles in two and a half hours; it was a blessing that we were returning safely. We would have been drowned.

In just half an hour we were berthed and passengers began huddling down in rain.

God blessing, we returned all alive. And back in hotel rooms we freshened up and made a beeline for the dining hall. Happy. However, Bimal hoped tomorrow would not be like today. I warned him : Not a single word for Havelock, please. We've had enough of it.

The same evening we did not go out. It was raining but the storm had waned much. Bimal was restive; he wished he would still see Havelock if the weather permitted. He phoned the competent authorities for information about the possible departure of the ship. But, to his dismay, he learnt for two days the port would remain closed.

Then I intervened to say, 'Forget about Havelock, let it remain a distant dream.'

Next morning we decided to visit the historic Cellular Jail, ill-famed for solitary confinement and brutal torture of Indian freedom fighters by the British rulers. The stains of blood the hounds had sucked out of the lynched torsos could not be noticed but the stink had not fully evaporated. After buying entry tickets we requisitioned the services of a woman guide to show us around. As we saw the museum we had a patriotic feeling by looking at the pictures of the brave souls but when we had to see the barbaric scene of torture on a replica of the fighting spirit we fell sick.

Coming inside we went to the view-tower from where the wings of the jail had spread. Originally, there were seven wings but now only three, which survived the bombardment by the Japanese invaders during the Second World War. On the wall of the tower there were marble plaques on which are written the names of the freedom fighters. The Bengalees top the list followed by the Punjabis.

The long corridors of the jail wings which had survived the Japanese attack are negotiable, and the guide took us along them telling the story about how a detainee was kept confined in one cell with the iron-rod window placed high above near the ceiling and the steel-fenced gate in the front kept under lock and key, thus separating one prisoner from another.

On the corridor of one wing just facing down the gallows we walked and found at the end the cell of Veer Savarkar with his scribblings well preserved on the walls. Sometimes he was kept standing within a fenced verandah to watch how a condemned prisoner would be taken to the gallows for the last rites. Along with other prisoners the Veer would sing *Vande Mataram*. Kissing the rope thus became a divine ritual.

Netaji Subhas Chandra Bose once visited the jail, which has now been converted into a national memorial. And near the gate a memorial column has come up. In the middle of the memorial compound is placed a white tablet on which is written a long tribute to the fighters of independence, but unfortunately the word 'independence' has been misspelt as 'independance'.

The same evening we witnessed Son-et-Lumiere in the open pavilion of the jail, but the saga of freedom fight, though brought us virtually alive, appeared to be disjointed. My mind was left vacant.

One day, in the meantime, we had a lavish luncheon at Piku's house. Another night we were guests at the dinner hosted by a Bengalee couple known to Bimal.

We would never forget that night. We had gone there by taxis, but on our way back home we did not get the transport as we had expected. Late as we were in coming out the of friend's house we got stranded on the road running along the shoreline, its waves sparkling and glistening with moonlight. Not a single cab could be seen. We started walking , washed and cooled by the sprinkles of sea water. A hotel came by. Suddenly, feeling the divine blessing within, a taxi was spotted. We waved our hands and asked the driver to stop. The driver did not oblige us then. He said. 'There're passengers for the hotel. Please stop. I'm coming.'

Within a few moments the taxi arrived. Besides the driver there was a helper. So all of us could not be accommodated in one cab. Bimal, Badhan and Tushar pushed me in and in the backseat Sabita, Rita and daughter, and Usha were huddled. The driver asked the three of our party left behind to wait. He said after dropping us in the hotel he would come back to reach them home.

Our taxi arrived in the hotel in a few minutes. I offered to pay the fare, but the driver refused to take it. Smilingly he said, 'Three of your team are waiting for me. I'm soon coming with them. Then I'll take it'. He left with the car. We sat down on the lawn washed by the moonlight. We were talking about the three left behind. Within minutes the taxi entered the hotel gate and stopped. Out came the three friends of ours. And Bimal paid the total fare.

The taxi driver did not take a rupee more than due. It was a human grace! A human life it was, but this life seems to surpass divinity. Or is it divine grace that manifests itself through the humanity? I kept my eyes shut and felt within me a kind of faint vibrations probably echoing the degree of others' feelings.

Another evening, might be the eve of our departure for our home city, the visit to the Marina Park newly built on the shore down the hill of the torture jail was a great pleasure. The park is all the time blessed by the lashing waves and cool breeze. Lights all over, some people were enjoying boating on the man-made backwaters of the sea.

Next evening, we the eight plus and our island friends met at a dinner jointly hosted in a hill-top Chinese hotel. The sky was moonlit, the hill a bit cool and the smell of the oncoming dinner just great.

We sat by a rectangular table, candle-lit and flower-bedecked, the Burmese-Chinese owner keeping a constant vigil on the arrangements.

Lobster and crab dishes were rich; chicken preparations simple yet palatable; and veg menus spicy.

We talked more than we ate, yet we ate more than we could. Overfed, we came out into the open with the still hazy moon sending down its goodbye bliss from the divine heaven. But what was about our divinity within? I went aside and meditated for a while and what I discovered was more than a shadow of the heavenly delight.

In the jumbo car of Bimal's friend we got in, we all—the eight plus, the two plus, and the owner who was in the driver's seat. With pleasing smiles pervading the interior of the vehicle we went up the hill, by the All India radio station, to a viewpoint from where we had a wonderful rendezvous with nature. Really, we had a grandstand view of Port Blair by night about which we did not have any idea. The U-shaped bay with lights blinking from surrounding houses looked like Nainital after sunset.

We bade a tearful farewell to our friend, the man behind the entire itinerary, but I personally felt it was too difficult to say a farewell to the love that was life that was divine.

Divinity is omnipresent

Early next morning we left for the Port Blair airport to catch the scheduled flight to Kolkata. An assistant manager of the hotel arranged a lift for us. Airlines official Subhankar Banerjee whom we had met at Jolly Buoy came and told us the flight would be a little late. The plane from Chennai had not yet come.

After check-in we were waiting in the departure lounge when Piku and Muniya entered. They, too, were going to Dum Dum.

The plane arrived roaring and taxied at the bay when passengers disembarked. Some time after we were asked to proceed to the plane. One the way I saw Pinaki standing at a distance. I waved my hand to him. And to Mr. Banerjee standing next to him.

Moving on the runway for a while the jet took off leaving behind the charming city of Port Blair and the encircling sea, invaded by green islands. Soon we were airborne. There was blue above, there was blue below, and in the vacuum in between the plane was flying fast.

For an hour and forty minutes the plane flew through the mid-air. Then we felt it was losing altitude. Beneath us we could see the Ganga Sagar and deltaic regions of the Sunderbans, the green and green with river-alleys drawing wonderful dividing lines.

Soon after the plane flew over Salt lake—Science City, the stadium, and Vidyut Bhavan. And then the smooth touchdown at Dum Dum.

Out we came, the eight plus, into our heavenly abode on earth. Was this not homely happiness and bliss infinite? All divine?

14

TENSIONS ALL

Tensions all, all the time, and it was my life. I could never conceive of any tension-free phase. But why was it my constant companion? Were these uneasy perturbations pre-ordained?

Every birth has its pangs, so has every death. And these pangs were creative of tensions. Did I then inherit the tensions my mothers suffered at the time of my birth? What would happen when I would die? The same kind of tensions, then, isn't it?

But one good thing would then happen—I would leave behind me all my tensions. Will my posterity then suffer from them? Won't they overcome them?

It was not unnatural, as is the case with most human beings, that my life would have ups and downs on the way to maturity and ultimately death, but the magnitude of my problems too many increased only my tensions.

In my childhood days, when I was too young to understand what was happening around me, I fell prey to odd tensions. My mother died in her prime. We were two brothers, the third one having died earlier just after my mother's death, adrift uncared for in the ocean of fathomless fear, a total void never filled in. My father preferred to remain a widower for the rest of his life. That way we had the divine bliss, getting all love and affection and care of my father.

My student life was seldom tension-free. Before every

examination, be that in the school, college and the university, I would have nervous twitches, my hands trembling when I got question papers, my forehead sweating as I started answering them, and my sleep deceiving me during the intervening period till results were out. And before the finale I would slip away from the city. When my matriculation results came out, I was away in my village home. I was out of station when my I.A. and B.A. results were published in gazettes.

So did it happen when I got my M.A. results. Far away from home. Only the results of the LL.B exam came while I was home.

The early period of my married life was nowhere near the freedom from tensions. Only social work I used to do, though at times tensions grew up even while engaged in philanthropy. Nothing positive I did that would help me earn the livelihood. My wife Usha did not pester me with innuendos but did neither spare me the warning. And she feared I was doing politics in the guise of social service. I could not convince her about my well-intentioned social manoeuvres. Again my tensions increased with my increasing family. Even petty issues often led to uncompromising acrimony.

Being born in a village I had a feudalistic upbringing for which I faced several difficulties in surmounting the emotions and sentiments associated with the worn-out system.

However difficult it was to make adjustments with emerging new way of life, I was not done up. The socialistic orientation of my mind helped me a lot to get out of the rut, relieving much of the traumatic tensions I was in.

Yet I could not claim I had become a different man, having a thrust for democracy. Somehow I had thought the futuristic model of life would be democratic through the mixing of the dying feudalism-cum-capitalism and the upcoming socialism.

The only fear that haunted me all the time was the nuisance of bureaucratic overlordship which might ultimately destroy the foundation of the newer social fabric.

Since I was undecided in taking up the right path to basic freedom, I did not have the proper authoritative control over inexplicable tensions. I looked for an alternative but to no effect. Being in a dilemma I had to remain satisfied with illusions.

As a budding journalist I paid much of my attention to learning the tricks and techniques of the profession. All in seriousness, keeping away from my commitments to society, but in the beginning of my career I was a little half-hearted, for which there was no easing of tensions.

Later, however, my involvement in journalistic pursuits became engrossing and unwavering. Any kind of professional lapse, even though unwittingly done, made me nervy. I did not try to explain away failures; I faced the music in the morning-after post-mortem. My social work done with courage gave me a good fighting spirit. Often coupled with divine understanding I did brave the weather. And no regrets.

My sons and daughter gave me much of the tensions, their education, their employment and their marriage all the time keeping me on my toes. However, they fared well. By and large. I was much freed of tensions when they were well settled in life. Only the severe illness of my younger daughter-in law aggravated my tensions seemingly beyond control, but the inner strength born of my divinity within got me back on the rail.

Whatever my divine perceptions, I did not become a diehard. With the run-up to divine realization strictly keeping to the right track I could overcome odd hurdles to reaching the goal of democratic enlightenment.

I had developed left leanings in the socio-political environment, but as I always tried to avoid petty-fogging in politics I placed myself miles apart from polemics, and the kind of aloofness I had nurtured helped me out of the wood when disenchantment took many of my friends offguard. Still my patriotic tensions presisted, even if the 'do or die' movement launched by Mahatma Gandhi ended in mass arrests and the escape of Subhas Chandra Bose from India brought a massive uprising during the INA trial but failed to prevent partition.

We stood almost helpless when refugees were coming in torrents from the other sides of the border. Our tensions only grew; we built up improvised shelters for them in my village; but it was the irony of fate that they did not stay for long in the shelters but went away to take refuge on the platforms of railway stations. We used to feed them but now they lived on doles. Later, by means of forcible occupation of lands near the heartland of the city they built camps and colonies. But did that ease tensions?

No, my tensions did not abate. Wild thoughts had been plaguing me about the unfortunate people in camps and mushrooming colonies. Would they be herded again into sacrificial altars? Political self-seekers and money-spinning brokers were about.

A new addition to my tensions occurred when the government acquired our landed property. Virtually this loss of property on which our family was a lot dependent for the livelihood pushed us to the brink of poverty and hunger. My father was then too old to face the ordeal, and we the two brothers, with our paltry incomes, were in a spot. We did not get any interim relief, and, to our dismay, we got the compensation money after a long fight for twenty years, when my father was no more with us.

We were down but not out. I stuck to my profession of journalism, though not a money-bag. My brother left the village to join the government health service and, later, got a better job in the Durgapur Steel Plant. Once all such developments dispirited us; our family was in disarray.

Struggling quite hard though, to make both ends meet, a kind of hellish megalomania overtook me. The earth to me appeared morbid. Not heavenly. Yet, as luck would have it, my divinity within did not leave me, because of manifestations now and then.

The girl of bubbling beauty I had loved and married was an old woman still working for hours to maintain our family balance and keep safe distance from doom. We seemed to be on the rocks, both of us.

'We shall overcome' But when? Tensions did not seem to leave me. Only occasional blessings came to me. As once it happened at Ranchi, at the conference on 'Reporting Chhotanagpur'. Before I started speaking extempore. I sought divine blessings; and they came. I came through.

The divine bliss helped me draw applause even from the elderly media persons who had been felicitated at the conference.

As I took to teaching after my father's death, I felt happy. Teaching was in my blood. But initially my tensions shot up. Entering classrooms and delivering lectures to an intelligent audience told on my nerves. Seriously then I got down to business and overcame my tensions in a big way.

Tensions were agonising in my journalistic job, but soon my ingenuity in news editing and newspaper making helped me get along. My inhibitions gone, I gradually rose to the height of a philosopher even though I taught a hi-tech subject like editing.

For lack of Indian-authored books containing indigenous illustrations I often faced difficulty in explaining even basic problems. This prompted me to write books that would suit Indian students. My books sold, since they properly highlighted the two-way traffic between technology and techniques.

Tensions prevail in other spheres of my life, too. Today, as much as they existed yesterday.

Iddle talks or just innocent gossips sometimes were life-giving, and I was fond of them; but they turned into quarrels oftentimes. Perhaps, the lifestyles of today give little scope for incessant talkathons. Fast life must have eroded leisure, the prime motivation behind them. And without this kind of mental food for thought my tensions only worsened, resulting in narrow-mindedness. For diversion I constantly endeavoured to form laughing clubs, but all in vain. Laughing is happiness divine.

Individual characters were important in the business of laughing. And for divine manifestations a deep-rooted revolution of such characters was necessary.

Swami Vivekananda talked of this element of individuality in human character. And particularly so when he dwelt on socialism as a better alternative to existing governmental systems, providing a solid bedrock of divine love that manifests the equation of man and man and, if possible, the communion of man and God.

The socialist camp led by the Soviet Union blatantly ignored this spiritual individuality as the basic element of socialism and went in for regimented humans, generating sort of rigidity that boomeranged as morbid dogmatism dismantling the very social fabric idealised for decades. Swamiji wanted to go the Vedantic way of man-making to establish socialism on the basis of real egalitarian democracy.

My tensions increased because of our failure to dispel the inner contradictions inherent in imposed socialism.

All my life I tried out this way of divine flourish but I could not say for sure how much successful I was. Never did I want to be caught on the wrong foot. So I was off the beaten track.

Tensions left me in the lurch when my intense love for music and song died young, for reasons beyond my control. I was lucky to have the company of friend Nemai Chand Boral, who became the head of music both at Viswa-Bharati and Rabindra Bharati. Once, at a function Nemai accompanied me on the harmonium when I sang two of Salil Chowdhury's songs which brought me overwhelming clappings. My silent tears increased only my tensions.

Another day, maternal uncle Nutubehari Chatterjee came to our city residence and sang two devotional songs. After him, I sang a modern song. He said my voice was good but was at a hairline distance away from the *sargam* tune.

In utter anguish I kept off music. I forgot to sing, I only hummed. I thought I had better involve myself in earning our bread. Because of my self-imposed embargo on my musical propensity I turned a non-singer.

Singing makes life divine, I am denied the bliss.

Tensions reigned supreme. Often.

From being to becoming would remain a useless exercise. Mostly for me, who was ever tensed. Divine ethos seems indefinable.

15

EARTHLY THOUGHTS

An old man of the world as I am, I can inoffensively look for my heavenly elevation at one go. There is nothing wrong with this common wish, but nobody knows if it will so happen. What I can say for sure is my lift-off to the starry heaven will be an impossible hat. My feet touch the earth, which is near to the eyeshot of both – heaven and hell. Will then it be my straight or wavering lift-down?

A laughable question it is, and I swear there is no answer to it.

It is stated in between the heaven and hell the earth runs as the equator thereby maintaining an equidistance between the two extremes. But is that true by any stretch of imagination?

My optical periphery, too, is not expansive enough to give a correct idea about how far away is the heaven or hell from where I stand.

Is the heaven high up in the sky? I wonder.

Is the hell down under the sea? Again I wonder.

People generally look up to the great Himalayan heights to locate the heavenly abode and seek out the hellish legion down in the bed of the Indian Ocean. Do they find out what they want to see? No, in either case. They just wander about aimlessly.

My sensibility – is it not blessed by spirituality? – goads me near to the eternal truth that this mother earth holds both the heaven and hell.

Whoever is born on earth, dies, and he is born again, with a recycled life. There is no end to the life process, the death being the interim pause. All is earthly. And within the parameter of the earth there appears the heaven and the hell in eternal co-existence.

It is a utopian thinking that the two extremes are poles apart or that they are two parallel lines never to meet, portraying an either-or picture. The substantive essence of the two is correlative, one living alongside of another, forever being 'two-in-one'.

My mind is a peculiar idea in my body, invisible yet inviolable, seemingly an impregnable perception that in my body anatomy there is something non-sensual; and what I deign to say is that whenever I am in difficulty, I call to mind the heavenly hand in overcoming it, but queer it may sound that I do seldom seek the hellish help.

Who else does want the hand of the Hades while in difficulty? But it is also true when one seeks divine blessings it is the hand of the heaven, armed with the passport of the hell, is extended to the seeker. Such is not always what happens. Sometimes the blessings do not come, what then? The hell takes over. This is what we may call the absolute togetherness of virtual opposites.

Is it a kind of equation? I do not know the answer for I am poor in maths. And let the philosophers argue if this kind of discovery is absolute.

Four events I can relate when I could arouse the divine spirit within me. And all the four were born of tensions.

The first one was virtually an accident. It occurred on the road. But I was saved, my life was spared. And, certainly, behind my life was the divine hand.

In the early seventies, along with my daughter Tanima, I was crossing the busy Rajabazar junction, near Sealdah. It was office time, so the traffic jam was formidable.

We were going to a college on the other side of the road to get my daughter admitted in the BA honours course there. We got down from the bus and stepped forward to cross the wide road. The traffic was then at a standstill as the policeman on duty had raised his hand. We were in a hurry, since the admission had become a problem and I was too tensed to be alert about the traffic.

We made safely for the divider of the road on which tramlines were laid, but the moment we put our feet down on the road to cross the other half of it the traffic was on. Suddenly, an old automobile came over me. By then Tanima had crossed over to the pavement. I could not, and I was about to be run over.

I did not know what had propelled me to bend over the bonnet of the car, still then speeding though slowly, and hold on to it. Tanima had covered her face and cried out. I was then literally back-running holding on to the bonnet and this continued for moments. For how long I did not know. Only thing I remembered, I was then praying to my divine spirit for life.

Finally, the car stopped; by then some metres had been covered, me hanging on to the bonnet. There was a hue and cry. But I could not hear it as I was in a rage and ran to the driver to lob a blow on his face. Just then I saw an old man on the back seat sitting dazed, bewilderingly sorry. He pleaded with folded hands for forgiveness. Still I argued why the driver had not used the brake. The old man said he had, but it was a mechanical brake.

I was still standing on the road trembling, my face blue with fear.

The second one I have reported early, in brief. Way back in 1966, I was touring West Germany, when my plane developed trouble mid-air over East Germany. From Hamburg I was flying to West Berlin. It was dark below, a few lights blinking, faintly. Airborne though, passengers, me included, were feeling ill at ease. Why? Had something gone wrong? Just then the captain announced on the speaker that the jet was losing altitude too often.

'Pray to God', he declared.

All aboard the plane went pale. Heads down they were praying to God. I for myself put my trust in my divine spirit within. A few jerks and jolts after; all was quiet and the flight became trouble-free. The crisis blew over with our plane touching down safe.

The Berlin city is on the earth, I realised it is a better place than heaven to live in.

Mother Adyasakti of whom Sri Ramakrishna had spoken in the *Kathamrita* and whom I revered much since my school days, once saved us – Usha and me – from the third problem that made us shake in our shoes. Away in Bangalore, where we were on a short visit from Chennai.

The entire day following our arrival night in the city we spent at the Tipu Sultan town of Mysore seeing majestic sights including the eerie lights of Vrindaban Gardens. At two in the afternoon next day we were to catch the Vrindaban Express for our onward journey to Kolkata via Chennai the same night.

On arriving at the Bangalore station we came to know none was allowed to travel by the express without prior reservation. Ignorance was no excuse. The man behind the counter refused to give us tickets. Already thirty-eight passengers had been waitlisted.

We were in a soup. I asked Usha to sit down with the luggage. I made a dash for the station superintendent. He was out. It was lunch-time. Yes, it was past one-thirty and only half an hour left for the train to start. I came back and told Usha I was going to meet the chief commercial officer. Upstairs I hurried and the CCO was good enough to make inquiries, but he was dismayed. There was no silver lining. Coming downstairs I found my wife was in tears. I asked her to pray to Adya Ma. She said she had been doing it. It was fifteen minutes left. I lost no time running upstairs. I stood before every desk praying for two tickets with reservations. Frustrated I came down to see Usha all through weeping. Only ten minutes to two – I saw my watch. Again I climbed the stairs breathless and as I walked up to the CCO he was kind to me and told me to wait for two minutes as my saviour would be coming. I looked at the wall clock. I was literally sweating.

'Parthsarathi, come here. A friend is waiting for you.' Another man on the other side of the table by the CCO shouted at my saviour. A handsome betel-chewing man came to me with a smile.

'Tickets? No reservations?' He took a breather, but I was about to lose my breath. It was only five minutes to two when the train would whistle off.

Parthasarathi asked me to follow him. We went downstairs. 'Where's your wife?' 'Down there,' I said pointing to the place where she was sitting. On the way down he heard the story of my predicament.

'Follow me, you both, with luggage.'

The gatekeeper did not say anything. Parthasarathi asked my wife to wait in front of the booking office. He took me to the TTE incharge and requested him to accommodate us in the train. 'They are journalists, came to the conference and are to return to Kolkata by tonight's Madras Mail.'

'O.K. Buy them tickets.' The TTE incharge sent with us his junior. On the way to the booking office I handed to Parthasarathi the fare. Usha was in tears, still.

Patthasarathi returned with two tickets in hand. We then took the luggage and proceeded with him, the TTE assistant following us. We stopped before a coach just behind the pantry car. With the tickets in hand we boarded the train and sat on two front seats, as directed by the assistant.

The train moved. It was just two. The TTE man also got up. And Parthasarathi, the saviour appearing as Lord Krishna, waved at us. We waved back. And soon he went out of sight.

It was the divine grace; the divinity within me thus manifesting itself in a manner I would ever remember.

Dame Luck was divine enough to save us from sure death in high seas one morning during our tour of the Andaman and Nicobar Islands. We had planned to visit the Havelock Islands about forty miles away from Port Blair, but our voyage by the mid-sized ship Ramanujam (I have briefly referred to this earlier) was disrupted by the eyclone turning violent and mercilessly battering the ship in which we were in. We had covered only a few kilometres from the shore when fear struck us that there would be ship-wreck, a disaster that would lead to the watery grave of so many people on board.

We had dreamt that we would enjoy the surfing on the widely known Radhanagar beach, but the dreams remained unfulfilled for ever. And Bimal, the leader of our entourage, got hurt so much that he kept on harping on the theme of a visit to the islands any day any time.

In spite of the bad weather, and as there was no ominous forecast in hand, we went out of the hotel in the big wet and when we were in, sitting comfortably on the couches by the wide glass-covered windows of the deluxe. cabin, we could not think of such an impending disaster. The captain giving the signal, the ship moved away from the port, but me suddenly felt the ship had begun to toss and tilt sideways, this side touching the waves while that side the blues. And vice versa. Often did we hear cracking sounds at the bottom of the ship. We feared the ship would split into pieces, or would capsize into deep burials.

Except Usha, me and Tushar, all our friends and the hundreds of passengers got sick and started vomitting, flooding the floor. Some lay fainted or almost dead.

Strange convulsions were a horrible sight, the big hall of the ship turned into a hospital. Usha held my right arm tightly and then left me to sit with Sabita only to come back soon. Sabita was head down. Badhan had moved to a sofa to recline. Tushar lifted Rita and placed her on a long bench on which she tossed constantly to and fro. His daughter lay on his tired lap. Sima was ill, from the moment the ship had left the shore. Bimal left her, sat on a narrow bench holding a pedestal fan and started vomitting.

I remained sitting on my seat looking out and as I felt giddy I started counting waves for diversion.

A little earlier I had tried to get coffee for all my teammates. But I could not make it. The stall-holder had fled. One boy got me two or three glasses only. But while reaching cups to Bimal and Tushar the ship tilted wildly and the hot liquid fell on a sleeping man who got up startled and fell down asleep.

The astern of the ship was just a few feet away, and as I was making desperate efforts to remain steady I put up a brave face and ventured out. The deck was empty, the violent wind sweeping away whatever was on it. I looked at the turbulent sea but I dared not lose my grip on a solid iron pillar. If I did so I would be thrown overboard, into the hissing sea. To my horror I found an old nun from Kerala struggling to remain seated and then to move inside. She looked pale; her face damp, and was fiercely trembling with fear.

I prayed for divine strength. Holding tight the iron pillar I stretched my fractured right hand out to her. Immediately she caught hold of it. With all my energy gathered I pulled her. She got up. And as I dragged her, she fell down near my feet. She sat down and with folded wrinkled hands prayed, 'Oh! God' With much effort I crawled into the cabin, she following me, soaked and shaky.

The ship appeared a plaything of the funny weather which had erased the demarcation line between the heaven and hell. Usha was dumb. Silent. She must be praying to Adya Ma. I held her. Are you steady?' She just saw me. Dazed. I sat by her. Moody.

Suddenly, some black oily slush fell on our seats from the air-condition openings in the ceiling of the ship. My dress was spoiled, so was Tushar's.

The hefty captain entered the virtual graveyard and after taking a look around went away. And then came the breathtaking announcement : We're returning to Port Blair. It was godsend, and all at once sat up. An engineer who was then passing by told us : We've covered only a few kilometres and can't proceed further.

The 'hero' of the fourth episode, Havelock played havoc, almost. We were near the hell. Now back on earth we were all smiles.

Somebody quipped, 'Are we in the heaven?'

'No. We're very much on earth we live in.'

Unquestionably, this was my realization as well. And for this realization the innermost divine prowess of mankind generally waited in the wings. As I thought it, all combined exercises of the divinity within had generated a universal democratic love which could prevent the disaster.

A childish inference, no doubt; but the broadness of my mind resulting from the divinity culture as I do it was certainly behind my pervasive democratization required to wish everybody good. And the good really came to all of us as a bliss. Indeed, a humble follow-up of the thrust for the human equation.

But I am not that much egotistic, neither too much elated in thinking of my inherent power No, I do not possess any such strength of mind. But what helps me tide over several crises is a subjective process that often flowers into an objective force motivated by the democratic saviour.

This participative philosophy of life is all that I try to hammer home, because through this way only man can go with man and even beyond man where man is one with oneness.

My perceptions being simple, modest and enterprising I do have little faith in silly pretensions or ivory-tower sermonising. An in-built aversion to bluff though I have, I do not fight shy of calling a spade a spade. This is courage which, I think; helps my unfoldment.

The divine activism whatever of mine is based on empirical observations punctuated by applied equations and the philosophy so developed is humanism far from the madding egocentricity. The entire process of orientation towards a character revolution has greatly freed me from spiritual inhibitions and ritualistic fetters. And blessed I am in stepping boldly towards a democratic dimension of socialised personality.

This is the divine spark. I try for its ignition in me. And I get now and then its feel.

Am I not one with it? Am I not all with it?

EPILOGUE

Pearls and pebbles picked up from here and there of the personal file of my seven-decade-long life in this mundane world represent how much care has been taken to build up my case for divinity within. It is a story, if not history, of the discovery channel I have followed to justify what I want to say.

All my searches within me for divinity have not led to successful discoveries for all the time, since several have been cases of failures, where divinity has befooled me by remaining elusive, but there is hardly any scope for questioning the propriety of my efforts at achieving revelations.

The wide-ranging yet intensive survey I have made for long shows how many manifestations of the divine self there have occurred and how many pleasures there have been eyefuls of the bliss, although I would not claim I am a superior person endowed with an extraordinary gift that is godly. What I humbly say I am one of the common run but with a difference, the difference being I have the kind of insight which many people do not have.

Admittedly, my work betrays some autobiographical touches delineating the ups and downs in my life which only indicate the successes and failures in a journey on an uneven terrain, yet all the years I have been through I have tried to keep to the right lane steadfastly moving towards the divine light.

The world around is fast shrinking today constantly battered by depressive ideas born of sheer isolationistic narrow-mindedness turning the universal system of human equation into a vast junk of impurities.

For lack of understanding what divinity within is about and

how it has manifestations in everyday life this hellish mound has blocked the way largely to the ultimate discovery of the divine horizon.

From being to becoming is not an easy process of human development; whether material or mental, but my philosophy of life has remained one of humble researches into the core of the brain-heart-stomach trio for the real unfoldment of divinity. I could not claim the core of my within has fully come to light but something has happened that would be enough to put man on a par with man, if not beyond man.

My picking up pearls and pebbles from my personal file is never intended to prepare a message of life for my sisters and brothers on this mother earth to follow. Still I have a message of living for all of us, but that is the message of love which would result from deviating from the path of material self-seeking and by rising above the petty egocentricity. Man is a being who has to undergo becoming, and this is the central theme of divine love I want to convey as a message to the genre of the new millennium. It will be my pleasure if anyone of the new genre emulates in one's own way what my message stands for and to that extent my discovery volume will be a success. Let every life bloom into a divine halo.

Never have I been a full-fledged political being, but my hobnobbing with some champions of left-oriented politics has given rise to certain unwholesome misconceptions diluting even my proneness to social work, but one good thing that was, was the development in my thinking that regimented socialism is a flop while a democratic building of individuality based on man-personified socialism is the divine flourish ahead.

Mine is not the futuristic model, but the spiritual bent of my mind flowering with an emboldening feat worth the while, despite the introspective overtones, is not a bluff but is good enough to bring forth the chorus of 'one with oneness'

The pearls and pebbles picked up in earnest are but stepping stones to the world of divinity making humanistic happiness infinite.

INDEX